Pr

The Language of Disciple-Making

I am happy to applaud the effort of two colleagues who are now leading The Bonhoeffer Project. Bonhoeffer taught us that the German word for "discipleship" meant succession. If you don't have new disciples, many new disciples, who succeed you, then the entire system that Jesus gave us backs up like a blocked water line. I laughed out loud at the great stories they told. I liked the simplicity of their approach in dealing with the meaning of language and word with clarity. I know that both men, working lead pastors, have moved forward in the implementation of what they have written. I want you to read this, and part of the good news is that it isn't War and Peace. I tried to read that and I failed, I tried Moby Dick, and failed. You can read this and succeed, after all, wasn't that Bonhoeffer's point, you succeed when you have successors, some call them disciples.

- Bill Hull, Author Conversion and Discipleship: You Can't Have One Without The Other and Co-Founder of The Bonhoeffer Project

Words are of little benefit unless they are clear. So much of discipleship depends upon understanding the truth of Scripture. But you cannot apply the truth of God's Word without clarity and intentionality with your words. In The Language of Disciple-Making, Dan Leitz and Jim Thomas provide a wonderful book that makes familiar biblical words clear and precise. This book will help you be a better disciple and make better disciples.

- Sam Rainer, President, Church Answers

I recommend this book by Leitz and Thomas to everyone, especially church leaders who need to think through and capture key definitions and concepts in disciple making for their church or ministry. We spent important time working through some of the concepts (definitions) in this book with national leaders at discipleship.org (see discipleship.org/about-discipleship-org).

- Bobby Harrington, Pastor, Author and CEO of discipleship.org and renew.org

DAN LEITZ AND JIM THOMAS

THE
LANGUAGE
—— OF ——
DISCIPLE-
MAKING

SAYING WHAT WE MEAN ABOUT DISCIPLESHIP

The Language of Disciple-Making:
Saying What We Mean About Discipleship

© 2022 Dan Leitz and Jim Thomas
© 2022 Bonhoeffer Press

ISBN 979-8-218-07109-7

Bonhoeffer Press
Oceanside, California

Printed in the United States of America

This book is dedicated to the faithful brothers and sisters in Christ who make up the National Leadership Team, Regional Representatives, Cohort Leaders, and participants of The Bonhoeffer Project. May God bless you as you pursue "world revolution through local movements of disciple-making by turning leaders into disciple-makers".

CONTENTS

PREFACE

Dan Leitz

My grandparents on my mom's side would visit for a month or so from their wintery home in Minnesota when I was younger. Living in California my whole life, I had never understood what real cold was like as a child. My grandparents would always tell me of below zero temperatures which would boggle my mind and make me thankful that I lived in California. My grandparents were midwesterners through and through and had all of the telltale signs of midwesternism in their language and mannerisms. Growing up, we had our fair share of "You betchas" and "Don't cha knows" in my household, as my dad was from Indiana and got in the midwestern game from time-to-time as well. I grew up with my mom making a mean "Tater tot hotdish," and we only had "pop" in my house, not soda. Many of these phrases and sayings weren't all that weird as I had grown up with them as commonplace in my home. It was only awkward when my friends stared at me whenever I used these phrases and "isms" outside my house.

I can specifically remember one year when my grandparents came to visit. It was a typical January in Southern California, and both of my parents had gone to work that day. I woke up feeling ill with a stomach bug and needed to stay home from school that particular morning. Since my grandparents were there, my mom and dad could still go to work while my grandparents watched me at home. As I got out of bed, looking for some pop or something else to settle my stomach, my grandma said something that, to this day, I will never forget. She uttered from the living room, "If you aren't feeling well, maybe you should just go lay on the davenport." That isn't a typo, and you are not alone if you have never seen that word before. If you have, you are probably from the Midwest. Well, being from southern California, the term "davenport" had never been registered in my memory banks. So, not feeling well, I immediately began the process of going through my mental Rolodex of terms and seeing if any of them fit. Never finding a mental match, I did the only thing that my ten-year-old brain could think of; I started to infer what it could mean logically. Now you may be thinking, "Why didn't you simply ask what she meant?" For starters, I was sick, and secondarily, my grandma said it with such conviction and vigor that I must know what it meant. I began to work through the word logically. My grandma said to "go" lay on it, so it must be somewhere else. She also said to "lay" on it, so it must be flat. The only thing that I could come up with is that my grandmother must have told me to go lay on the porch outside. Port/porch, you can see where my ten-year-old brain was. So, I grabbed a blanket and a pillow and headed out, thinking that my grandmother must know some unique midwestern trick where the cold SoCal January air would help my stomach.

I went outside and proceeded to get as comfortable as possible while lying on the cold concrete outside my front door. I was a compliant kid, so I thought I was doing the right thing. About 15-20 minutes after I went outside, I began to hear my grandma yelling for me. I started yelling back at her because I knew that she was a bit hard of hearing. She came outside and looked at me wrapped up on the porch with a look that can only be described as bewilderment and shock all rolled into one. She snapped at me, "For cryin' out loud, what are you doing out here?" I proceeded to let her in on my logic and confess that I didn't know what a davenport was. She then explained that a "davenport" was a sofa...a sofa. "Why didn't you just say that in the first place, Grandma?" She began to tell me that, in her neck of the woods, a davenport was a brand of sofa that became a synonymous term for a sofa or a couch.

As I look back today, I see this whole situation as a hilarious misunderstanding that demonstrates a broader truth. We can talk to each other, speak English words, and never completely understand what someone is saying. In my example, confusion over a term that I didn't understand, and one that I didn't intentionally seek to understand ... instead I guessed. What Jim and I desire to accomplish in this book is to expose the need for a more intentional focus on the language we use when it comes to disciple-making. It is amazing to think that with all of our advancements in technology and information, we are actually losing ground when it comes to the words that we use, along with their meaning. Without intentionality, we have different definitions in our heads that make it seem like we are talking to one another, understanding one another, and going in the same direction, when in reality we are saying words and completely missing what is being said.

We intend to take you on a journey in this book. To be clear, this journey comes in three parts and with a warning.

Exposing the Problem

The first part of this journey, and probably the most challenging part, is exposing the need for clarity and intentionality in our language as it applies to disciple-making. My grandma, bless her heart,

11

used a regionally accepted word that had no meaning or relevance in my world. What she took as commonplace and understood, I saw as confusing and ultimately worthless. Her intentions were good, her heart was in the right place, but I was literally out in the cold because of a lack of understanding. The truth is that there will not be a single word that we will present that any Bible-believing, God-fearing person wouldn't agree with. The words are familiar, but what we mean by them is not always clear. This is what makes it so vital to expose this problem. Because none of us will disagree with the importance of these words and their value to the discussion of disciple-making, or even Christianity as a whole, it makes it all the more imperative that our language be precise, intentional, and clearly understood. This is where the warning comes in.

In order to expose the problem and how it has permeated the Church and its culture, we need soft hearts to receive what is being said. 1 Peter 3:8 admonishes us to have a "tender heart" and a "humble mind." We will need both of these working together because, when something like this is exposed, it is often hard to see. Not because we don't see it in an observational sense, but because we *don't* want to see it in our own lives. We will need to overcome our pride barrier to see clearly what the Lord intends to point out. As we begin to dissect these words and expose how the definitions have become convoluted, murky, and lacking intentionality, our natural tendency will be to rebuff what is being exposed and not see the corrective work that we pray God wants to do.

Evaluating Our Language

In the second part of our journey, we will encourage everyone read-ing to begin the process of evaluating the current language used in your specific context. Had I employed this step with my grandma, I would have never been out laying on the concrete on a cold January morning. This means asking ourselves and others good questions that will get to the bottom of our language. It means that we have to be highly intentional if we want to make any headway into clearly communicating through language the things that God intends us to communicate with one another. The process of evaluation screams for intentionality. Even the psalmist, in Psalm 139:23, says to God, "Search me, O God, and know my heart! Try me and know my thoughts!" This is the psalmist crying out to God for accountability and the understanding of ourselves! We must ask God and others to evaluate us, the words that we use, and the intentions of our hearts. The bottom line is that our evaluation is self-accountability. This process of language evaluation should include questions like:

- What do I mean by this word?
- What do others hear me saying?
- What do I assume people know about this?
- Am I clear about my meaning?

All of these, and more, are questions we must be willing and able to ask and wrestle with if we are to make headway into this critical subject.

Implementing Language Change

Once we have exposed the problem and examined and evaluated our language, we must work through implementing language change that will get us on the same page with those around us and help us pursue disciple-making with clarity. Now hear me clearly, we are not going to be just providing new definitions for common words that have already been defined. We will, however, because language is constantly evolving, have to adapt our language to a changing world. The world we live in today is a world that is constantly changing, and our language must adapt as we try to convey different messages throughout different cultures, times, and seasons.

Some of you reading this may not think this is necessary, but let me give you an example that makes this step essential. Take the word "silly" for instance. Most of us, upon hearing this word, think we know what it means. However, I will tell you that it depends on when you hear it, or in what context and time in which it was written. The word "silly" has an interesting etymology. The word started out in the early 1200s with the meaning of "happy" or 'blessed." Yes, you read that right. The word then changed over time from "happy" or "blessed" to "pious," to "innocent" (late 1200s), to "harmless," to "pitiable" (late 1300s), to "feeble in mind, lacking in reason, foolish" (1570s). We must be intentional about implementing language change, as we need to make sure we are clear in our communications and pursuits.

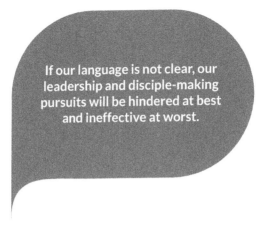

If our language is not clear, our leadership and disciple-making pursuits will be hindered at best and ineffective at worst.

We must be intentional about crafting definitions that will convey what Jesus called us to do; we must be clear about how we are calling others to follow us as we imitate Christ (1 Corinthians 11:1).

We genuinely hope this book will be a resource for you and your whole team to re-establish the use and intentionality of the language God has given us.

INTRODUCTION

Jim Thomas

Life goes by fast! I can remember it like it was yesterday. My oldest of two daughters, now in her early twenties, was just a toddler at the time. She had just started to formulate words and connect those words to specific objects in her small reality. One day, we were going about our normal routine and I heard the words that I had been longing to hear. Or so I thought. With clarity and excitement, she shouted out with all her might, "Da-do!" My heart leaped! Finally, she had acknowledged me as her father and used language to express her love, appreciation, and veneration for the one who had given her life, provided for her every need, and protected her from the wilds of the wicked world. She had finally seen me for who I was, God's called man to love and raise this child into a life of maturity and adulthood. I would be the one whom she would look up to, whom she would seek to emulate, and of whom every male in her life would be compared. I was her "Da-do!"

It was about that time that my wife, whom God has gifted with the ability to keep me in line, humble, and on track, spoke with all the patience she could muster, yet with an air of humor underlying her words. She gently pointed, and said, "You do know that 'Da-do' means 'dog,' don't you?" My heart was broken! My dream was shattered! I knew she was right, seeing the canine usurper close by, but I wasn't ready to admit that what I thought was reality simply wasn't. I wasn't willing to concede that my precious little girl had chosen her language to express her awe and wonder over a dog instead of her dad. Now, to be clear, that all changed as she grew older. My dreams have come true and she, as well as my younger daughter, think I am the best dad in the world (or so I keep telling myself, but denial is a powerful enemy). And what about the dog? Easy. We bought cats!

Language Is the Currency of Life

We were formed by language. Fourteen times in Genesis 1[1], God uses language to create the light, the night, the sky, the earth and the seas, the vegetation, the sun, moon, and stars, the animals in the sea and on the land, and finally, his greatest creation, mankind. In other words, language is literally the act of creation. Just as God spoke, when we speak, we are participating in the act of creation. Not that we are physically creating things *ex nihlo*, but with our language we are creating ideas, identities, perceived realities, and context for living life.

We are sustained by language. Whether verbal or nonverbal, all of us operate daily by the use of language. In other words, we move through life based on language. Over the past 10 years, the church I serve has partnered internationally with church-planting and disciple-making movements in several countries. It is amazing how different those experiences are based on language. When we take groups into countries like Brazil, we are definitely out of our element, as most of our group doesn't speak Portuguese. But because of training in English, Spanish, French, or German in middle school, high school, or college, some words, either spoken or written, can be understood, and in some situations, context can even be discerned without an interpreter. Our partnership in South Korea is totally different. As westerners visiting an eastern culture, language becomes a significant barrier, if not a nonstarter. Outside of Seoul, or other large cities, where some signs are written in English as well as Korean, any attempt to read or speak the language is futile. The symbols of language are different. The intonation of the spoken language is different. Without help, we are simply lost.

We are connected in relationship by language. Relationships are fostered and matured through language and broken apart by that same language. Whether it is toddlers agreeing to play together or fighting over a toy to adults agreeing or disagreeing on marriage, parenting, work, faith, politics, or sports, we relate to one another through language. In fact, as much as language is the currency of life, it is also the jet fuel of relationships. Think about marriage. Every marriage book, conference, video, or training I have attended over the years emphasizes the key role of communication in healthy marriages. With healthy communication, marriages thrive; without healthy communication, marriages implode. As such, words matter. One word, or group of words, spoken out of context, without definition, or with a contrary tone can send a couple into a deep relational hole. On the contrary, intentional words of love, encouragement, respect, and fidelity can lead a couple to marital health and happiness. Obviously, there are more factors to a thriving marriage than just language, but it is a key determiner of health. This truth can be applied to any and every human relationship possible. Language is simply the fuel of relationships.

We create worldviews by language. Language expert and professor Lena Boroditsky says, "The beauty of linguistic diversity is that it reveals to us just how ingenious and how flexible the human mind is. Human minds have invented not one cognitive universe, but 7,000."[2] The old axiom, "you are what you think," rings true. Our worldview, or how we perceive the world around us and live in it, will be directly affected by the language we embrace. Even King Solomon, in Proverbs 23:7, says, "For as he thinks within himself, so he is."[3] How we interpret the world will always be shaped and formed by the thoughts we think and the language we use to express those thoughts. The words and symbols associated with such thinking will then create the larger context for a group of people and will direct their actions toward specific objectives and goals that line up with their way of thinking.

We form societies and cultures based on language. As thinking and language help to form worldviews in individuals and groups of people, societies and cultures are then formed around the ideals and desires produced through that language. It is in the context of these societies and cultures that life is then lived on the ground. It is where we eat, sleep, work, and play. It is where relationships are formed around common interests and goals and flourishing, or conflict exists as those goals eventually evolve or change, and the language with it. Have you ever heard someone lament that it is no longer "the good ole days" or that "this family, church, town, etc. just isn't the same anymore?" Well, in one sense, they are correct. Time marches on and things are not the same as they were (age, technology, morals, etc.). But in another sense, "the good ole days" were probably not that good, given that we have lived in a fallen world since Genesis 3. I would contend that the positive reflection on the past has more to do with preferred thinking, language, and actions that, through the course of time, have now changed. As such, the new version of culture has become unpreferred to that certain individual or group. Therefore, when thinking and language change, individuals or groups either push back against what they perceive to be unhealthy changes in culture, adapt to new thinking and new or updated language, or create new thinking and language to help move people, organizations, or cultures into a new day of health and growth as a society.

Language As Disciple-making

So, how does all of this relate to making disciples of Jesus Christ? Well, just as there is language attached to all of life, there is language attached to disciple-making. The language we use regarding disciple-making will determine our theology of discipleship, as well as our practice of discipleship. In fact, language is a key to creating disciple-making cultures in churches and ministry organizations. Faulty language breeds faulty discipleship. Intentional and purposeful language creates disciples-making movements that produce faithful disciples who are obedient to Jesus' command to "Go, therefore, and make disciples of all nations, baptizing them in the name of the Father and of the Son and of the Holy Spirit, teaching them to observe everything I have commanded you."[4]

This short book is not about the language of being a disciple of Jesus. There are many wonderful books out there on such a topic. They help us to understand not only what it means to be a disciple of Jesus but what characteristics and actions are to be taken as one. Our goal is to move beyond the descriptive nature of being a disciple to the progressive nature of making disciples. As we do, language is key!

So, where are we headed? Well, no doubt by now you have looked at the Table of Contents, as I usually do when I begin a new read. If not, we challenge you to do so now. Each of the words represented help to form a language of disciple-making. As you work through the admittedly familiar ideas of gospel, disciple, vision, culture, change, plan, implementation, multiplication, evaluation, and perseverance, we hope that you will both bring your preconceived assumptions regarding these words and an openness to the table as we investigate them individually and how they relate to one another. As we do, our hope is to craft a more holistic view of what it means to make disciples in Jesus' name, and help you hone a specific language of disciple-making that is biblical, memorable, and reproducible in your local ministry context.

So, let's talk.

CHAPTER 1

GOSPEL

Dan Leitz

The gospel. The Good News. In Greek, *euangelion*. The apostle Paul called it "the power of God for salvation" in Romans 1:16. Whatever you call it, I love the gospel, and I am sure you are reading this book because you love the gospel too. The reason that we must start with the gospel is simple: everything flows from it. The Apostle Paul correctly states in 1 Corinthians 15:14, "And if Christ has not been raised, then our preaching is in vain and your faith is in vain."[1] Paul is telling us that if we get the Good News of Jesus wrong, everything that flows from it will be wrong as well. If we don't get the gospel right, nothing else downstream even matters.

Now, I know what you must be thinking (because I thought it too), "How can we mess up the gospel? How can anyone mess up the Good News? I'm a pastor, and the gospel is what I do." Well, it's easier than you think. Several books, as of late, are pointing out this problem in our modern churches. In the very first chapter of Bill Hull's book *Conversion & Discipleship*, he outlines six false or incomplete gospels that are preached every weekend across the globe in our churches. Scot McKnight, in his book, *The King Jesus*

Gospel, said, "I believe the word *gospel* has been hijacked by what we believe about 'personal salvation', and the gospel itself has been reshaped to facilitate making 'decisions.' The result of this hijacking is that the word *gospel* no longer means in our world what it originally meant to either Jesus or the apostles."[2] In his book *The Divine Conspiracy*, Dallas Willard referred to many of the gospels preached in our churches today as "The gospels of sin management." These great thinkers and writers have put their fingers on one of the most significant problems in the modern church age. We forgot the core of the gospel. We forgot to tell people to follow Jesus.

Exposing the Problem

In my early days as a Christian, full of religious zeal and idealism, I would often preach the gospel to strangers wherever I would go. It wasn't uncommon for me to have a conversation with someone in the grocery store checkout line or with someone sitting next to me on a plane. I have always been an outgoing sort of person, and in many cases, I was able to strike up a conversation with a perfect stranger in a very non-threatening way. One particular day, while flying somewhere for ministry, I was wearing my usual loud "Jesus shirt", which would instantly cause people to pray. Now, they wouldn't pray in a good way, but rather that they wouldn't be seated next to me on the flight. I would find it funny how many people thought it would be weird to sit next to me, given the aggressive nature of my t-shirt.

The woman I was seated next to that day was in her late 40s and looked to be coming home from a long weekend bender with her friends. I immediately struck up a conversation with her, which I gently steered toward the spiritual. Seeing as she was giving details about her wild nights over the past weekend, I knew that hitting her up with the problem of sin would be prime conviction material. I started into my usual spiel about sin and her need for a Savior, giving what I thought to be a clear and concise presentation. It must have been, because within moments of sharing the Good News about forgiveness and heaven, she asked me what she could do to be forgiven. "Got another one," I thought to myself. I told her to pray and ask God for forgiveness.

As I prepared to seal the deal and walk her through a sinner's prayer, she looked at me and said the words I will never forget, "And then what?" I asked her what she meant, a bit shocked. Again, she asked, "What do I do after asking God for forgiveness?" I looked at her, quite puzzled. In all the times I had shared the gospel, I had never been asked that question. The only thing that I could think of was telling her to find a church and "get plugged in." Seemingly unsatisfied with my response, she slumped back in her chair and put on her headphones. After all, she didn't pray the sinner's prayer or make any profession of faith. She was stuck on what happens *after* the prayer, and I was stuck on why I was having a hard time answering her.

Bill Hull highlights this problem when he says, "I realize that speaking against preaching a simple gospel that addresses our need to get to heaven is not popular. And to be clear, I believe there is a place for this type of presentation. But it should not be the norm for preaching because this reduction of the gospel is lethal to the church and its mission. Since our purpose is to be disciples and to make disciples, nothing matters more than our understanding of what it means to be saved. Jesus is counting disciples, not decisions. If we attempt to grow Christlike disciples with a flawed gospel, we will fail."[3]

In his book *One.Life: Jesus Calls, We Follow*, Scot McKnight, states bluntly, "Here's our problem today. Not only do we not like ultimatums, but we have too many Christians who have accepted Jesus into their hearts and who have been baptized and who have confessed their sins and who have joined the Church and who are in Bible studies and who are absolutely 100 percent convinced they are going to heaven, but who are not followers of Jesus. There are many who haven't made it real. The mark of a follower of Jesus is following. The mark of a follower of Jesus is that she or he has given Jesus her or his heart. It's that simple. It's that demanding. It's that serious. Jesus was a moral zealot and he expected his followers to become moral zealots too. He wanted them to live the Committed. Life."

For me, this begs the question, how did we get here?

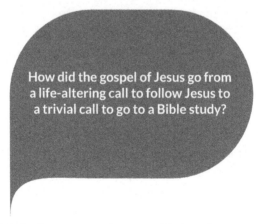

How did the gospel of Jesus go from a life-altering call to follow Jesus to a trivial call to go to a Bible study?

A while back, I was watching an old clip of a pastor giving an invitation for people to follow Christ. It was a standard gospel presentation that gave people the option to give their lives to Christ. The preacher repeatedly said, "Will you accept Jesus as Lord and Savior of your life?" I didn't think much of it at the time because it was something I had said before, and I didn't find it particularly notable. A few weeks later, I listened to an even older preacher on the radio. Towards the end of his message, he also began to give an invitation, but his invitation was a bit different. He asked the audience if they would surrender to Jesus. It smacked me like a ton of bricks. One pastor asked people to *accept* what Jesus had done, and one pastor appealed to the listener to *surrender* to what Jesus had done. Accept Jesus or surrender to him. Though used interchangeably in many gospel presentations over the years, the words have a significant difference in their meaning and understanding. It sent me on a journey of sorts, and I began to look back into recent history and noted a subtle shift in the 1950s and 1960s from gospel presentations slowly replacing the word surrender with accept. It was almost as if it was a purposeful effort by pastors to water down the call Jesus gave. That moment gave me some much-needed clarity on the words that I use and the intentionality of the words that I choose.

To expose this problem means that we must admit that most, if not all, of us have failed at one point or another to preach the gospel in its fullness. We have failed to tell people to follow Jesus. As I look back today, I know that what I was preaching to that woman on the plane was an incomplete gospel. I was preaching to her a forgiveness-only gospel. I was telling her how to get to heaven instead of how to follow Jesus. Today, in churches across the world, pastors and laypeople alike continue to ask people if they want to go to heaven or if they want to be forgiven. That incomplete, "what's in it for me" kind of gospel has been preached in many western churches for the better part of the last century, and the result is a Church that is more anemic than ever, and lacking in the work and power of the Holy Spirit. If we are going to see a paradigm shift in the

Church in our lifetimes, we must reclaim the discipleship gospel that Jesus preached, and we must shout it from the rooftops with clarity, intentionality, and without compromise.

Evaluating Our Language

As the gospel is at the core of Christianity, you would think that defining it is something easily done by almost every Christian. Unfortunately, it is not. I'm not saying that people haven't heard the word gospel before, or don't have a general knowledge of it. I'm simply saying that the meaning of this important word is missing, or at the least incomplete, from the minds of the average church-goer. If I gave a 3x5 card to each of you reading this book, and I asked you to define the gospel, I would get all sorts of responses. Most of them would hover around the same general definition, but none would be the same. Some might say, "It's the Good News." Some might revert to Sunday school and simply say, "Jesus!" Others might say, "Salvation." Some people would get closer and talk about repentance and the death, burial, and resurrection of Jesus. However, because this word is so rich and its implications so vital, it would seem that we need to make sure that the intentionality surrounding this word is clear and known. There is much more to say on this subject, which is outside the scope of this book. For a more detailed definition, I recommend reading *The Discipleship Gospel* by Bill Hull and Ben Sobels.

Let me illustrate why it is so important not just to get the meaning of the word close to correct, but to understand, proclaim, and define the word gospel with biblical accuracy. A few days ago, Jim and I were headed to Orlando for a conference where our organization, The Bonhoeffer Project, had a booth and a few break-out sessions. As we left the hotel, Jim was at the wheel of the rental car, and I was sitting shotgun. These positions in the vehicle have vital roles, especially when you are not familiar with a city. Jim's responsibility was to drive the car as safely as possible, according to the rules of the road. My job was to provide him with the directions for getting to the church where the conference was being held. As we left the coffee shop where we made a pit stop, I opened the navigation app on my phone. I scrolled to the previous addresses I had used the past couple of days, made my selection, and let the turn-by-turn navigation voice do her thing. It was a short 20-minute drive with traffic to the conference, so we settled in for the drive. About 18 minutes in, I noticed that the scenery didn't look familiar, and the buildings around us looked much taller than I had remembered. As I looked down at my app, I quickly zoomed out to see where we were. To my dismay, we were in downtown Orlando instead of the conference location, which was about five miles in the other direction. Desperate to find out what went wrong, I looked through my phone and realized that I had inadvertently selected the city of Orlando, Florida, instead of the exact address of the church where the conference was being held. I quickly changed the address, and we eventually got to our destination, albeit a few minutes late.

This story, although frustratingly funny, demonstrates how being off by just one exit, one unintentional fat thumb click, can lead you to the wrong destination. We had a car, the address, and turn-by-turn voice navigation. We had fuel, our backpacks, and all the material we needed for the day. We even had the best intentions to get to the correct destination at the right time, and safely, but we were off. This is precisely why we *must* be accurate in defining the gospel we preach, teach, and proclaim. Even when we have the best of intentions and all the right tools around us, it is possible to lead people to a destination that is altogether different than our intended target. In his book *Conversion & Discipleship*, Bill Hull says, "The gospel we preach, determines the disciple we produce." We must define the gospel and evaluate and examine the gospel we proclaim and teach to ensure we know it and communicate it correctly. And here is the kicker, we may have the correct gospel in our hearts and minds, but what do people hear us say? As a pastor, I often have people come up to me after a sermon and say, "I loved when you said (insert crazy thing that never came out of my mouth here), and I said no such thing. It is critical for us to examine our gospel, evaluate it against Scripture, and proclaim it accurately to make sure the people we lead arrive at the intended destination.

Looking back on that day with Jim in the car, it was completely obvious to anyone with whom we spoke or came into contact that morning that we had the best intentions of getting to our ultimate destination. It shows us the need to evaluate and reevaluate. It was not simply enough to have the means to get to our destination (the car, the drivers, road safety). It is not enough to have the ability to plot a course toward our destination (navigation). Much to our dismay, it is not even about having the right heart or intention to get to the proper destination. Only when all of these are working in unison, and there is a constant stream of evaluation and re-evaluation, can we even hope to reach the proper destination. Had I not looked up to see that the road and surroundings didn't match the intended target, we may still be driving around Orlando, or beyond, looking for the final destination.

Implementing Language Change

Mark Twain famously wrote, "The only person who likes change is a baby with a wet diaper." We resist change because it involves work and takes us out of our comfort zone. However, failing to act now will only prolong the issues and make the work down the road that much more challenging. Let me share with you a famous story about the Kodak company which illustrates why waiting to take the necessary steps toward implementing change can ultimately lead to unintended and disastrous consequences.

Back in the 1990s and early 2000s, Kodak was the juggernaut film company that outpaced all others when it came to photography, cameras, and film. In fact, in 2005, Kodak's stock was more valuable than Apple, Inc. Kodak was the big kid on the block and had cornered the market on all things photography. Kodak resisted the change to a digital business model for far too long, and by the time they realized it, it was too late. In 2012 they filed for bankruptcy. They went from the top of the market to the bottom in seven short years, all because they were too slow to adopt change.

Implementing language change in many circumstances can involve slow and intentional changes over time that will eventually create the intended culture shift. In fact, I will argue for slow and methodical change later in this book. However, we cannot be slow in getting this one right or slow in adopting clear and intentional language as it pertains to the gospel.

> We cannot wait any longer to expose, evaluate, and implement the necessary change in our lives or our churches.

Kodak thought slow would be ok, but unfortunately, their failure to act quickly was their downfall.

Let me give you one more story that will illustrate why acting now is of the utmost importance. Several years ago, when I was the technical director at my church, I listened to my former senior pastor give a sermon that used quotes regarding some famous Christian missionaries who died while proclaiming the gospel. Being the technical director, I spent most of my time in the main sanctuary listening to every sermon from the sound booth. In this particular message, he read a quote from a book that said one of the missionaries had succumbed to "jungle fever." Now, there are two types of people who just read that. There were two types of people in the audience that day as he read the quote. Those who understood what he meant, and those who were confused, and possibly even mortified. Some of you who just read that felt what I felt in the pit of my stomach that day. For those in the dark, let me bring you up to speed. The term "jungle fever" was a term used for decades to describe a malaria type of disease that, if left untreated, could result in high fever and even death. In my day, being a bit younger than the average age of attendees at church that day, *Jungle Fever* was a movie written and directed by Spike Lee that brought a new meaning to the phrase. The new definition of "jungle fever" spoke of a romantic relationship between an interracial couple.

Three-quarters of the congregation heard that this missionary died of malaria, and the other quarter heard that he died of an interracial relationship. To this day, I still laugh to myself every time I think of that situation. It is funny now, but it wasn't then. As soon as I heard him utter the phrase, I became instantly concerned. I began scanning the room to see who understood and who was confused. From the side conversations and the giggling happening amongst the younger attendees, I could see that the phrase was lost on many. After that service, I quietly and quickly pulled him aside and told him the double meaning of the phrase he had spoken. He was equal parts dumbfounded and mortified. Needless to say, in the following services that day, he changed the word to malaria; no one misunderstood and no one was the wiser. He didn't hesitate in adjusting his language. We both knew that the potential for confusion was tremendous, and that confusion would result in many people not understanding what he was trying to communicate. So, he changed his notes immediately. The following week he even spoke to that service again to offer clarity to the words he had used.

These examples should motivate us to implement language change and not wait until it is too late. Change at this level of importance cannot be slow and will take leadership, perseverance, and may involve conflict to accomplish. It will also take humility and the ability to apologize if what has been communicated has been off or needs to be clarified. It may mean that you may have to go back to basics and do a sermon series on the gospel. It may mean that you have to get over your pride and admit, like I had to, that although my intentions were good, I had not been as thorough, biblical, and intentional as I should have been. This cannot wait until later. Jesus said it himself, in John 9:4, "We must work the works of him who sent me while it is day; night is coming, when no one can work."[4]

The practical side to all of this is being able to answer some basic questions about the gospel you are communicating to others. I invite you to prayerfully answer the following questions as an individual, a leadership team, a church staff, or any other gospel proclaiming capacity you may be involved in. My recommendation is to ask these questions with at least one more person in your context. It is my experience that having another set of eyes on these questions and inviting someone else into the process is critical for your to get an accurate answer to the questions below.:

    a. What am I currently saying (as it pertains to the gospel)?

    b. What are people hearing?

    c. What am I inviting people to do?

    d. Does the gospel I proclaim make a certain kind of disciple? Is it the kind of disciple I intend on making, or that Jesus is calling me to make?

    e. Based upon the answers to the questions above, what needs to change?

CHAPTER 2

DISCIPLE

Jim Thomas

I am a lifelong Dallas Cowboys fan. Now, we may have just lost some readers with that statement, or may have found kindred football spirits, but regardless, hang in there with me. When I was serving in my first church as a youth pastor during my seminary days, a dad of one of my students approached me on a Sunday. I knew the man to be gracious and a hard worker. He worked for an elevator/escalator company as a repairman. Though I was aware of his vocation, I was unaware of the details of his clientele. He started the conversation by telling me one of his main clients was Texas Stadium, the then home of the Dallas Cowboys, where he had an office and serviced all the elevators and escalators. He then offered me an invitation. He said that if I ever found myself with tickets to see a Cowboys game, I should stop by his office to see him. Taking his offer at face value, I promised the next time that I was at the stadium that I would do so.

Several months later I received a call from my dad offering me two tickets to the Dallas Cowboys and the then Los Angeles Raiders pre-season game. The game didn't start until after church, so I graciously accepted the tickets and invited one of my male students to go with me to the game. Remembering the man's invitation, I planned to stop by his office once we got to the stadium. Upon arrival we inquired where his office might be and made our way there. We found the office and my friend sitting behind his desk. He was surprised to see us since we had not contacted him beforehand. He graciously invited us inside and we spent a few minutes catching up. As game time was approaching and we needed to make our way to our very upper deck seats, he said that he had a gift for us. Reaching over to his desk, he handed both of us a pass with a lanyard attached. He said, "These are all-access passes to Texas Stadium. You can go wherever you want in the stadium. Have fun!" A bit confused and amazed, I clarified by asking, "What do you mean by 'all-access'?" He said, "Exactly what it means. You have access to anywhere you want to go. The press box, locker rooms, field, etc." Not believing our ears, we clarified a second time only to receive the same answer.

Leaving his office, we were still in disbelief. This is my team. This is America's team. This is the Dallas Cowboys, and we now have access to their world? It was too good to be true. That said, I looked at my companion and said, "Ok. Let's go to the locker room." His eyes widened in fear and disbelief, as if I had asked him to sneak over some international border to partake in espionage. I began to walk away, and he followed. We came to an elevator where a uniformed, walkie-talkied individual stood guard. With all the confidence I could muster, I showed him my all-access pass. He nodded, said, "Thank you," and we proceeded into the elevator. Mission successful! Well, at least partially successful.

We made our way down into the tunnels under the stadium and eventually found ourselves outside of the Cowboys' locker-room.

Now, this just wasn't any Cowboys team. This was 1991. The Cowboys were moving from worst to first in the NFL. They were on the brink of winning three Super Bowls in the 1990s. This was the era of Jimmy Johnson, Troy Aikman, Emmitt Smith, Michael Irvin, Jay Novacek, Nate Newton, and a litany of other superstars. Standing outside the locker room, we dared go no further. About that time the doors slammed open, and the team ran out. What I had observed on TV or in the stands all my life, the white jerseys, silver pants, and classic silver helmets with the iconic blue star, was right in front of me. Football hero after football hero piled out of the locker room. In a state of fervor, I spotted Michael Irvin and yelled, "Go get 'em, Michael!" To my surprise, Michael turned around to see who was yelling at him, and with the quintessential symbol of all masculine communication, he gave me the head nod. My heart leaped! I had spoken to one of the greatest receivers in the NFL! I was in the tunnel! I was part of the team! They will probably call on me to go into the game at some point!

Coming back to reality, we found ourselves standing in the empty tunnel reveling in the experience but wondering what to do next. My companion suggested we make our way to our seats in the upper deck to watch the game. At first, I thought to agree, but then remembered that we had all-access passes. All-Access! I said, "Well, we might end up there, but let's go on the field first." He looked at me like I was out of my mind. Not only had I invited him into espionage, but now he was acting like I was asking him to risk his life. I started walking away and he followed. When we got to the field, coming out of the tunnel the team had just exited, I looked around. A little hesitant to press my luck and go over to the sidelines, I saw two folding chairs leaning against the famous blue wall that surrounded the field. They were probably meant for some

THE LANGUAGE OF DISCIPLE-MAKING

sort of security personnel, but being that none were present, and because we had all-access passes, I grabbed the two chairs, set them up at the back of the endzone, and sat down. My companion joined me, though visibly nervous. We watched the first half from these seats, at times being as close as 20 yards from the action on the field. Eventually, we tired of our vantage point and moved to other parts of the stadium to watch the rest of the game.

When we left the game that evening, after a disappointing 17-12 Cowboy loss (eh, it was preseason!), we knew we had experienced something we would never forget. We were invited into a place that few fans had gone. We walked hallowed halls. We spoke to insiders, both players and staff. We watched the game from a perspective we had never known before. We were a part of something bigger than ourselves and were changed by the experience. We were forever marked by the invitation to participate in a world that was beyond imagination.

Exposing the Problem

In many ways, this is exactly what Jesus does when he calls us to be his disciples. He gives us an all-access pass to the Kingdom of God. But few understand or receive the larger invitation to this kind of life. They think that the Kingdom is some sort of esoteric thing that can't be grasped, or something to be attained only after death. As a result, they spend their lives sitting in the upper deck of the church, never stepping onto the field, much less having any effect on the game. The late professor and author Dallas Willard says that the key problem in churches today is a lack of discipleship. In other words, in most churches there is no sense of what it means to be a disciple of Jesus. He says, "Most problems in contemporary churches can be explained by the fact that members have never decided to follow Christ."[1] He says that because of this culture of "non-discipleship" in churches, we have opted for more of a conversionist mentality than that of disciple-making. The result is churches filled with people who have been brought to the starting line of faith without any indication of what new life in Christ really looks like (2 Cor. 5:17). Willard says, "Not having made our converts disciples, it is impossible for us to teach them how to live as Christ lived and taught (Luke 14:28). That was not part of the package, not what they converted *to*. When confronted with the example and teachings of Christ, the response today is less one of rebellion or rejection than one of puzzlement."[2] As such, most Christian leaders are inviting people to the starting line of faith, as we should, through evangelism and the promise of forgiveness and eternal life in Christ, but not much further.

In some ways this is a sort of "bait and switch." We say come to Jesus by faith, and that's all you must do to receive all that he has to offer. Now, this is not wrong, it's just incomplete. I had a member in my church say that he was told that all he had to do was pray a prayer to go to heaven and that's all that he had to do to be a Christian. He then asked, "What's with all of this 'follow me' and obedience stuff?" Again, this is not wrong, it's just a truncated form of the gospel Jesus preached that has produced significant consequences for the church (Mk. 1:15ff). Willard states, "More than any other single thing, in any case, the practical irrelevance of actual obedience to Christ accounts for the weakened effect of Christianity in the world today, with its increasing tendency to emphasize political and social action as the primary way to serve God. It also accounts for the practical irrelevance of Christian faith to individual character development and overall personal sanity and well-being."[3] This does not mean that Christians are not to participate in the political process or engage in social endeavors. But these are ancillary to who Jesus has called us to be as his disciples. It is the lack of personal and corporate obedience to what Jesus taught that is leaving the church spiritually anemic and creating a non-discipleship culture.

As a result, most pastors and leaders have not taken the time to intentionally map out a biblical definition of a disciple and all the implications of what that definition entails. If discipleship is to be our priority, and Jesus' main commission to his church, then the language of discipleship must be formed around the concepts of "the gospel" (Chapter 1) and "disciple."

Evaluating Our Language

So, what is a disciple? Great question. Jesus gave us the all-access pass when he said, "If anyone would come after me, let him deny himself and take up his cross daily and follow me." (Lk. 9:23, cf. Matt. 16:24, Mk. 8:34). Jesus' call to "follow me" as his disciple is one of a life-long commitment to transformative, spiritual growth and obedience to him. In fact, the Greek word for disciple in the New Testament is *mathetes*, which simply means "follower" or "apprentice." *Mathetes* is used throughout the Gospels and Acts (261 times) to designate those who actively followed Jesus. The last time it is used is in Acts 21:16. Following this verse, the writers of the New Testament employ several referent terms to describe his disciples. Examples include *believers* (Acts 5:14; 10:45; Romans 1:16; 1 Timothy 6:2), *Christians* (Acts 11:26; 26:28; 1 Peter

4:16), *brothers/sisters* (Acts 6:3; James 2:15), *saints* (Acts 9:13; 1 Corinthians 1:2), and *ecclesia*, or *the church* (Acts 5:11; 11:26; 13:1; 14:27; 15:3; 15:30; 15:41; 14:23; 20:17,28). But regardless of the term used, they all referred to those who Jesus would designate as his *mathetes*, or disciples. The bottom line is this: "All who are called to salvation are called to discipleship—no exceptions, no excuses."[4]

As stated in Chapter 1, this does not mean that we are saved through our obedience, but a disciple is one who lives in obedience because he/she is saved. The great reformer Martin Luther summarizes this idea when he says, "We are not saved by living according to Jesus' words, but by faith in what he has done. Yet anyone saved by what he has done will always want to do what he says. We are saved by faith alone, but not by faith that is alone."[5]

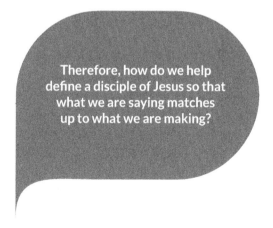

Therefore, how do we help define a disciple of Jesus so that what we are saying matches up to what we are making?

A biblical example will help us as we do the hard work of evaluating our language around the idea of a disciple. In Matthew 4, we see Jesus calling his first disciples. Matthew says, "While walking by the Sea of Galilee, he saw two brothers, Simon (who is called Peter) and Andrew his brother, casting a net into the sea, for they were fishermen. And he said to them, 'Follow me, and I will make you fishers of men.' Immediately they left their nets and followed him." (Matt. 4:18-20). There are several elements in Jesus' calling of his first disciples that speak to the calling and nature of a disciple today.

a. Jesus was actively calling others to himself.

Jesus actively invited people to follow him. Matthew says, "And Jesus went throughout all the cities and villages, teaching in their synagogues and proclaiming the gospel of the kingdom and healing every disease and every affliction. When he saw the crowds, he had compassion for them, because they were harassed and helpless, like sheep without a shepherd. Then he said to his disciples, 'The harvest is plentiful, but the laborers are few; therefore, pray earnestly to the Lord of the harvest to send out laborers into his harvest.'" (Matt. 9:35-38).

So, what was Jesus' central message? What was this "gospel of the kingdom" that he was preaching? In Matthew 3:2, he says, "Repent, for the kingdom of heaven is at hand." The kingdom of heaven is "the proclamation of the rule and Christ over all of life."[6] Therefore, Jesus was calling people everywhere to turn from their loyalty to their sin and themselves and turn and "follow him" (Mt. 4:19). Such turning involves a life fully surrendered to Jesus in obedience to his commands (Matt. 28:20; Jn. 14:15).

b. Peter and Andrew were actively doing something else.

At the time of Jesus' call on Peter and Andrew (and all the other disciples—maybe with the exceptions of Simon the Zealot and later the Apostle Paul), they were actively pursuing interests other than the Kingdom of God. In one sense, this is true of all that come to

Christ. Paul says, "And you were dead in the trespasses and sins in which you once walked, following the course of this world, following the prince of the power of the air, the spirit that is now at work in the sons of disobedience—among whom we all once lived in the passions of our flesh, carrying out the desires of the body and the mind, and were by nature children of wrath, like the rest of mankind." (Eph. 2:1-3). But when we come to Christ, we not only come into a new relationship with Jesus, we also embrace a new vocation. This is really what the Great Commission is all about (Matt. 28:18-20; Mk. 16:14-18; Lk. 24:46-49; Jn. 20:19-23; Acts 1:8). Of course, this does not necessarily mean all believers become pastors and missionaries, but we are all, by reference to Christ, called to take up a higher vocation. I have said it this way to our church:

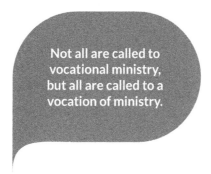

Not all are called to vocational ministry, but all are called to a vocation of ministry.

c. They responded to Jesus' call by faith and abandoned all else to make him the priority of their lives.

Given the invitation to follow Jesus, Peter and Andrew respond by faith and follow him. This is the invitation to discipleship.

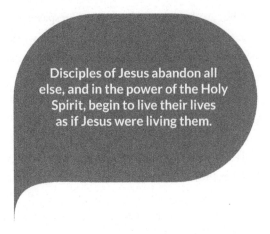

Disciples of Jesus abandon all else, and in the power of the Holy Spirit, begin to live their lives as if Jesus were living them.

Matthew says that "immediately they left their nets and followed him." Once they experienced Jesus, they knew their lives were never going to be the same. As such, they left everything behind to follow. The Apostle Paul would have the same reaction. He says, "But whatever gain I had, I counted as loss for the sake of Christ. Indeed, I count everything as loss because of the surpassing worth of knowing Christ Jesus my Lord. For his sake I have suffered the loss of all things and count them as rubbish, in order that I may gain Christ and be found in him, not having a righteousness of my own that comes from the law, but that which comes through faith in Christ, the righteousness from God that depends on faith— that I may know him and the power of his resurrection, and may share his sufferings, becoming like him in his death, that by any means possible I may attain the resurrection from the dead." (Phil. 3:7-11).

e. They were promised a better purpose in life.
In Mark's account of this story, Jesus promises Peter and Andrew that he will lead them into a better purpose than just fishing. He says,

"Follow me, and I will make you become fishers of men." (Mk. 1:17). Jesus would later say, "Truly, I say to you, in the new world, when the Son of Man will sit on his glorious throne, you who have followed me will also sit on twelve thrones, judging the twelve tribes of Israel. And everyone who has left houses or brothers or sisters or father or mother or children or lands, for my name's sake, will receive a hundredfold and will inherit eternal life. But many who are first will be last, and the last first." (Matt. 19:28-30). The promise of greater things is central to the call to be a disciple. In the Great Commission texts, Jesus is in the business of handing off his ministry to those who would follow him. He is, in effect, making his purpose our purpose. In fact, he says, "Truly, truly, I say to you, whoever believes in me will also do the works that I do; and greater works than these will he do, because I am going to the Father." (Jn. 14:12). As such, his disciples are to step into his sandals, with his authority, to accomplish his mission of new creation on earth, until he returns. This is the call to be a disciple.

Implementing Language Change

So, what is your definition of a disciple? Have you worked through all the complexities to make it clear and intentional? When my staff started to work through an intentional disciple-making plan for our church, we had to deal with this question. Our goal was two-fold:

1) For our team to all be on the same page with our language so that we are communicating the same thing to the congregation; 2) To do the hard work of moving toward a comprehensive definition that would be a framework in helping us craft a plan to make what we had defined. This took some time.

When our team came together to address the question of what

a disciple is, we brought decades of church experience, ideas, and even baggage to the table. As we started the process, I simply asked the question, "What is a disciple of Jesus?" Knowing that those around the table comprised multiple master's degrees and a few doctorates, the assumption was that this was going to be a pretty simple process. We were wrong. Over the course of many weeks, we struggled to work through Scripture, our denominational and personal church history, and what we desired to make in our current context. One of the greatest challenges was getting past the simple descriptions of what a disciple does to what a disciple is. Though the two are intricately linked, there is a difference.

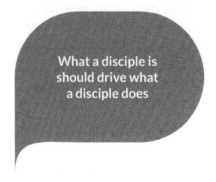

What a disciple is should drive what a disciple does

The problem is that we were trying to reverse engineer the process based on our observational experience. So, we returned to Scripture. We asked ourselves, "What is it that Jesus (and the New Testament writers) say that a follower of Jesus is?" This helped us to fetter through all our assumptions and come to a conclusion on a simple and intentional definition that would move us forward.

One of the key assignments in The Bonhoeffer Project is that we ask pastors and ministry leaders to work through the exact process

that my staff went through. Cohort participants are a̶s̶
through a biblical definition of the gospel and of a disc ̶ ̶ ̶ ̶ ̶ ̶ ̶
context. I clearly remember one participant (who has given me per-
mission to share his story), who had an outstanding and theologically
poignant definition of both "gospel" and "disciple." Any seminary
professor would have given him an A for his thoughtful and technical definitions. The problem was that it was so technical it wasn't very
transferable. He went back to the drawing board and came back with
a theologically solid, yet viral definition that could be understood by
the high school drop-out and the PhD in his church.

So, what are some key elements to the process of crafting a definition of a disciple? First, make Scripture your starting line. Don't
do what we did and start at the back end of assumption and experience. Ask the vital question of what Jesus and the New Testament
writers say a disciple is, then proceed accordingly. Second, gather a
team around you as you work. In other words, don't go solo. If you
want your definition to become viral, then build a team that will be
like-minded and will help with the transfer of the idea of a biblical
disciple throughout your entire church or ministry. Third, once
you get some momentum, revisit your definition considering how
Jesus made disciples. In other words, is the end of making disciples
being a disciple or making more disciples? One of the areas that
we see definitions fall short is in multiplication. We will talk more
about this in a later chapter but start thinking now about how those
you disciple will begin making more disciples and build that into
your definition. Fourth, "road test" your definition before rolling
it out. Run it by your spouse and children, some trusted leaders in
your church/ministry, some pastors/ministry leaders outside of
your context, even outside of your country, and get their feedback.
Finally, look at your definition again. Does it lead you to create the

kind of disciple Jesus has called you to make? If not, why not? If so, then you are on your way to creating or refining a plan to help you fulfill the Great Commission in your context.

CHAPTER 3

VISION

Jim Thomas

I stood on the top of a mountain in Breckenridge, Colorado in awe. I had taken annual snow skiing trips to Colorado over fifteen years, but it never failed to amaze me how stunning the Rocky Mountains are. If you have never visited the Rockies, or some type of similar mountain range, then you are missing a view of God's creation that, in many ways, is unapparelled on Earth. The scope of snow-covered peak after snow-covered peak is breathtaking. It is almost like looking into 4D cinema, seeing the color and depth of what is in front of you while feeling the cold wind and stirred snow hitting your face. It is dynamic, moving, inspiring, and a little frightening.

In many ways, such a setting makes you feel both big and small. It makes you feel big in the sense of being a part of something larger than yourself. Even up to this writing, when the topic of mountains, Colorado, or skiing comes up, I bear witness to my experience on top of that mountain. I want to tell people that I have been there and am the recipient of its benefits. I want to paint a picture for people of what I saw, heard, and felt, and I want to bring them into that reality, even challenging them to go and experience it themselves. In essence, I become a witness to something that is "other", something that can partially be described, but must be experienced to truly know. Conversely, when I talk to someone who has been where I have, there is a sense of solidarity, a sense of brotherhood/sisterhood based on a shared experience. Words like, "amazing," "awe-inspiring," and "overwhelmed" dominate the conversation as memories are stoked and the smallest detail is affirmed and championed.

But such an experience also makes you feel small in comparison. In some sense, it gives perspective to who you are and what you do. Any sense of arrogance is eclipsed by the grandeur of God's creation. The bravado of "conquering the mountain" is put on pause when the scope of your conquest is seen. David's words in Psalm 65:5-8 speak to this idea. He says, "By awesome deeds you answer us with righteousness, O God of our salvation, the hope of all the ends of the earth and of the farthest seas; the one who by his strength established the mountains, being girded with might; who stills the roaring of the seas, the roaring of their waves, the tumult of the peoples, so that those who dwell at the ends of the earth are in awe at your signs. You make the going out of the morning and the evening to shout for joy." Paul, speaking of God's general revelation to all people, speaks to God's grandeur in Romans 1:19-20. He says, "For what can be known about God is plain to them [the unrighteous], because God has shown it to them. For his invisible attributes, namely, his eternal power and divine nature, have been clearly perceived, ever since the creation of the world, in the things that have been made. So they are without excuse." Such awe-inspiring wonder, again, causes us to echo the words of David, "When I look at your heavens, the work of your fingers, the moon and the stars, which you have set in place, what is man that you are mindful of him, and the son of man that you care for him? Yet you have made him a little lower than the heavenly beings and crowned him with glory and honor. You have given him dominion over the works of your hands; you have put all things under his feet, all sheep and oxen, and also the beasts of the field, the birds of the heavens, and the fish of the sea, whatever passes along the paths of the seas."[1]

Even within the awareness of our place in the scope of God's creation, we may miss the bigger picture. God has revealed himself to us, through the general revelation of his creation as referenced in Romans 1, and more intentionally in the special revelation of his Son Jesus Christ, to invite us into a larger creation project. The whole story of God, the metanarrative of Scripture from Genesis 3 onward, is the story of God working to bring about new creation. After the fall in Genesis 3, we see God starting a process of drawing people back to himself. Through his provision for Adam and Eve to his covenants with Abraham and Moses, from the preaching of his prophets to the coming of Christ and the work of the New Testament church, God is in the business of restoring the world to himself. Jesus himself tells us of his mission. Quoting Isaiah 61:1 in Luke 4:18-19, Jesus says, 'The Spirit of the Lord is upon me, because he has anointed me to proclaim good news to the poor. He has sent me to proclaim liberty to the captives and recovering of sight to the blind, to set at liberty those who are oppressed, to proclaim the year of the Lord's favor.' As such, we see that 'Therefore, if anyone is in Christ, he is a new creation. The old has passed away; behold, the new has come. All this is from God, who through Christ reconciled us to himself and gave us the ministry of reconciliation...'"[2] In fact, at the end of all things, Jesus says, "Behold, I am making all things new." He also said, "Write this down, for these words are trustworthy and true."[3] In other words, God has crafted a grand vision for the world, the redemption of all things. He has invited those who have placed faith in Jesus to join him in his new creation project and has commissioned them to the work of reconciliation and disciple-making. But such a work can seem overwhelming, and many believers and churches have opted for something significantly less.

Exposing the Problem

In our experience with pastors and ministry leaders, very few churches have an intentional vision for making disciples. Most churches have a mission statement or some kind of general-purpose statement in their organizational documents, which may or may not relate to the Great Commission, but few have disciple-making as a key component for the future of the church. As such, making disciples falls into a subcategory of ministry relegated to a paid staff member to run programs, emphases, or campaigns, but doesn't help to guide the trajectory of the church toward a designated end.

One of my mentors, and a fellow partner in The Bonhoeffer Project, related a story regarding the tribe he belongs to in Christianity. Making disciples is proclaimed as the key ingredient in their denominational structure and local church work. In fact, this denomination was birthed as a result of intentional disciple-making. It is in their promotional material, on their website, and proclaimed as their purpose. My friend has served in this tribe for most of his life as a pastor and missionary and has seen the good and bad, as there is in any church denomination, network, or partnership. His observation of normal church life, though, has led him to a sobering conclusion. He says that even though disciple-making is stated as the foundation of their mission, he is not seeing disciple-making lived out in the vast majority of their churches. In essence, he says that they should be sued for false advertising!

Sadly, this tribe doesn't stand alone. Whether because of a faulty understanding of discipleship, faulty systems that don't produce disciples, or leadership who have little discipleship experience and therefore little passion for disciple-making, many churches lack any holistic vision for making disciples in their context. As such, they wonder why people are not growing in Christlike character and spiritual maturity, why they aren't reaching more people or sustaining membership and attendance over the long haul, and why the next "silver bullet" never seems to be *the* "silver bullet."

Thom Rainer, in his forward to Daniel Im's influential book, *No Silver Bullets,* says, "Church has become a litany of activities and busyness. It's become one program or one thing after another. And there's no intentionality or movement forward in a direction that demonstrates faithfulness with what God has entrusted that church. The solution isn't to look down the street and copy the nearby megachurch. Nor is it to blow everything up and start from scratch. And, by all means, staying the same is not an option either. There is no one silver bullet to turning around a dying church or continuing the growth of a healthy one. It takes several little improvements in different areas to add up to growth."[4] One of those improvements, though major in scope, is having a comprehensive vision for disciple-making.

Evaluating Our Language

It's a verse that we have all heard: "Where there is no prophetic vision the people cast off restraint, but blessed is he who keeps the law."[5] Theologian Tremper Longman III states that the Hebrew word for vision (*ḥāzôn*) comes from a verb (*ḥzh*) often used to describe a revelatory experience of the Old Testament prophets though it is also used for the simple act of seeing. In the previous verse, it is the latter.[6] The idea of "seeing" here can be understood in two ways: 1) Seeing the end goal in mind, or 2) The plan that is put in place to reach the desired end goal. The point of the text is that those who don't have an end goal in mind, or a plan in which to reach that goal, have nothing to direct them, and therefore stray all over the place. This is what it looks like to lack vision, and, unfortunately, this is what many churches and ministries look like in relation to disciple-making.

So, what does it look like to craft a vision for disciple-making in a local church or ministry? So many pastors, missionaries, or ministry leaders start to look at this question by asking two critical, but secondary questions regarding disciple-making. The first question centers around process. They want a plan to be put in place immediately that will facilitate making disciples or growing their church. In doing so, they avoid the hard work of evaluating, challenging, changing, and implementing language, and as such, end up creating processes that don't match up with their intended desires. The second question centers on curriculum or study materials. Though this is important down the line, let me make a strong suggestion here.

> If you haven't defined what kind of disciples you are trying to make and haven't set a vision for making them, then the curriculum really doesn't matter.

Sure, most discipleship curriculum is biblically based and good for study (though some is not), but does it match up with your intentional vision for your context? Does it fit the strategy you have in place to see disciples being formed over time? Does it add to or detract from the vision that God has given you? Will it really help point and direct people toward that goal? If not, don't use it.

So, again, what does it look like to craft a vision for disciple-making in your context? Pastor Tim Keller, in his book *Center Church*, says that every ministry needs to have what Richard Lints, Professor of Theology at Gordon-Conwell Theological Seminary, calls a theological vision. Keller states:

"...between one's doctrinal beliefs and ministry practices should be a well-conceived vision for how to bring the gospel to bear on the particular cultural setting and historical moment...Once this vision is in place, with its emphases and values, it leads church leaders to make good decisions on how to worship, disciple, evangelize, serve, and engage culture in their field of ministry—whether in a city, suburb, or small town...

Therefore, if you think of your doctrinal foundation as "hardware" and of ministry programs as "software," it is important to understand the existence of something called "middleware." So, what is a theological vision? It is the faithful restatement of the gospel with rich implications for life, ministry, and mission in a type of culture at a moment in history. Lints says, 'A theological vision allows [people] to see their culture in a way different than they had ever been able to see it before...Those who are empowered by the theological vision do not simply stand against the mainstream impulses of the culture but take the initiative both to understand and speak to that culture from the framework of the Scriptures...The modern theological vision must seek to bring the entire counsel of God into the world of its time in order that its time might be transformed.'"[7]

Therefore, a theological vision centered in disciple-making causes us to do the work of understanding biblical salvation, scriptural interpretation and reformulation, and current practices and methods. As we do, we begin to ask new questions around the ideas of the gospel, salvation, transformation, and obedience, and how we can apply it to every area of ministry life in the local church.

> Over the past several years, I have encouraged the leadership team in the church where I serve to see a theological vision as "a goal that is unreachable in this life but is worthy to pursue. Something bigger than ourselves."

In other words, what is it that we can challenge our ministry contexts to embrace that is bigger than themselves, gives them a sense of ownership, not only in their own discipleship but also in God's global work of new creation, and isn't something that will fade away when the new pastor, book, ministry fad, or program comes down the line?

Implementing Language Change

I am now a man of a certain age. With that comes the inevitable changes in physical health and prowess. This was realized a few years ago with a routine trip to my eye doctor. He informed me that around age 45, most people's vision starts to change. I have had an astigmatism most of my life. I wore glasses from college on and added contacts to the mix in my mid-30s. Overall, though, my prescription has not changed much, just miniscule adjustments over the years. That was until a few years ago. Even though I had not noticed a major change in my eyesight, after investigation my doctor informed me that I would need to move toward mono-vision contacts and progressive glasses. Balancing the fact of growing older with the new realities that entails threw me sideways for a little while. But when my new prescriptions came in, I realized the wisdom of my doctor's leadership. I could see better, especially with my progressive glasses. The glasses were "progressive" in the sense that the upper part of the lenses helped me see far away, the middle part of the lenses helped with my middle distance, and the lower part of the lenses helped me read things closer. It took a while to get used to them, as I was tripping over stuff the first few days, but once I did, everything changed.

Maybe we can look at crafting the language of vision in the same way. When we start the process of implementing language change regarding a disciple-making vision, we can see it like a pair of progressive glasses.

Top of the lenses

Again, the top of the lenses help us to see far off. Getting back to Proverbs 29:18, where does God want those he has entrusted to us to go? What is his vision for his people in your context? This is where the theological vision finds its footing. It's kind of like shooting an arrow or throwing an ax. If we do not have a target to shoot at, we will hit it every time, and people will end up aiming at the wrong thing or creating their own target as the goal. When a theological vision is put in place, then we can direct all our efforts as individuals and as a ministry toward that goal. Remember, a theological vision is "a goal that is unreachable in this life but is worthy to pursue. Something bigger than ourselves." At this point, you are probably wanting an example. Very well. The theological vision for the church where I serve states, "We want every member and attender to pursue a Christ-centered life. A Christ-centered life is living so that the personality and deeds of Jesus Christ naturally flow out of us wherever we live, work and play." We place this vision before our congregation in everything we do from church documents to preaching and teaching.

Middle of the lenses

The middle of the lenses help us to see where we are. Once we start to craft a theological vision, it will help us see clearly in the here and now. It is so easy to drift from God's call and vision for us and the ministry he has called us to.

I was in Panama City Beach, Florida several years ago. The new trend was renting a paddle board and going out on the water.

I thought this sounded fun, so I rented a board and a paddle and enlisted one of my daughters to join me in the adventure. Quickly tiring of the experience, my daughter made her way back to the beach, a chair, and a book. But I had spent $25 for an hour's use, and I wasn't going to waste that money. I battled and paddled for what seemed to be forever. Once I sensed my time was coming to its end, I looked up and couldn't find my family on the beach anywhere. In frustration I began to complain that not only did they leave me to my own devices but had gone back to the condo without me. I then realized that the condo I was looking at wasn't our condo. In all my efforts to keep myself upright and balanced, I had drifted a significant distance from where I had started. My family had not moved, I had.

Many of us in ministry find ourselves in this predicament. We establish mission statements, goals, and even processes, but over time, because of the minutia of management within organizational life, we look up and we are not where we are supposed to be. The vision hasn't moved, we have. Having a comprehensive theological vision that is placed constantly in front of leadership and those we lead helps to keep us from this drift.

Bottom of the lenses

The bottom of the lenses help us to see close-up. One of the problems in the life of organizational ministry is, as my dad always says, "keeping the main thing the main thing." We can so easily get in the rut of repetitiveness as we do the work of ministry. We fail to ask the critical question of whether what we have always done, or are comfortable doing, will lead to our stated goal. We also may fail to ask if our new, creative idea is just a new, creative idea or if it really leads toward our stated vision? The minutia does matter.

> Each decision we make should be in concert with our theological vision.

If it isn't, then we need to ask why we would add it to the process of what we are thinking and doing.

Finding balance

The key here is finding balance. If we are always looking far out, we won't be present in the moment with the vision God has given us and won't attend to the details. If we are always in the moment, we won't see the inevitable drift happen and will lose sight of our goal. If we are always looking at the details without incorporating them into the vision, or the vision into them, then we will be very busy, but unproductive in making disciples over the long haul. We must constantly see our theological vision for making disciples with the help of these "progressive lenses." When we do, we will find the balance we need and won't trip over our own good intentions.

CHAPTER 4

CULTURE

By Dan Leitz

Lit. Salty. Chill. Cool. Gay. Sick. Karen.

If you read any of these words and cringed a bit, you are not alone; I cringed a bit when writing some of them. The reason we cringed is that these words carry meaning in our culture. However, these words have different meanings for different people, at different times throughout history, in different contexts, and different cultures. Most of these words were innocuous in the past, as some still are today. However, over time, every one of these words has gone through a process known as semantic drift. Anyone with the name "Karen" may not be able to define semantic drift, but they have undoubtedly experienced it. Five years ago, anyone named Karen was just going about their lives thinking everything was fine. How could having a simple all-American name like Karen be bad? However, in the last few years, anyone with the name Karen has probably thought about legally changing their name to anything but Karen. Semantic drift is simply the evolution of a word and its meaning over time. Some shifts in a word take a while, and some changes occur very rapidly. "Lit" used to be something that you did to the wood in the fireplace, and now it means that something is "cool." "Cool" used to convey low temperature, and now it means "awesome" or "sick." "Sick" used to mean unwell, and now it means something amazing. "Gay" used to mean happy, but today it carries a different meaning altogether. All of these words have undergone semantic drift, and because of shifting cultures, changing politics, and shifting context, all of these words now carry different meanings than when they were first uttered.

I bring this up because there are words that have meant things to one generation that mean something else to another era. Think back to my story about the phrase "jungle fever" for reference. Because of the constantly shifting meaning of many words that we often use, we must look out for words that have undergone this semantic drift to catch them before adversely affecting the culture we are trying to create. But this begs the question, what culture are you trying to create? In order to create a new culture that is conducive to disciple-making we have to really get to the bottom of what a culture is and is comprised of.

Culture can be defined in several ways. Andy Crouch defined culture as "...what we make of the world."[1] J.R. Woodward said culture is, "...the combination of 'the *language* we live in, the *artifacts* that we make use of, the *rituals* we engage in, our approach to *ethics*, the *institutions* we are a part of and the *narratives* we inhabit [that] have the power to shape our lives profoundly."[2] I like to define culture as the way we do what we do shaped by the language, things, and people we do them with.

> The reason we must define this is because culture is everywhere around us and without intentionality the culture will define you before you ever get a chance to shape it.

Exposing the Problem

Language itself poses all sorts of problems, not the least of which is making sure we are on the same page with our definitions. I formerly taught logic and ethics in a Christian high school back in my early vocational days. One of the fundamental laws of logic that I would teach every semester is the law of identity. The law of identity simply states that something is what we say it is. These definitions make communicating and conveying ideas easier because we have an agreed-upon framework of thought, reason, and communication. The color red is called red because we all agreed to call the color we know as red, red. Think of it as a mental handshake we give one another as we communicate. Now, you would think that this is universal and that everyone would agree upon this fundamental principle that properly governs our communication and thought, but you would be wrong. We are wrong not in the words we use but in understanding the terms used and how that will subsequently affect the culture around us. You would think that standardized definitions would be immovable, and our culture would have had definitions and language arguments settled long ago. Wrong again!

Let me give you an example. Back in June of 2020, at the height of the civil unrest in the United States in the wake of George Floyd's death, Merriam-Webster decided to change the definition of the word racism. A word used for centuries that was universally accepted and understood for hundreds of years has been thrown out and changed. Now, I will not get into the back and forth over the reasons, but I found it fascinating that somewhere in an office building, a group of people decided to change the definition of a word. And it wasn't because there was a huge public outcry that demanded it. Instead, a woman from Drake university sent a letter telling the dictionary giant that the current definition was inadequate.[3] Did you catch that? Someone wrote a letter to an organization and said, "I don't like your definition, so you should change it." And they did. No one asked me if I was ok with it, and I am sure no one asked you either. I never saw a survey that asked the world if we think that the definition of any word should be changed, but they changed it anyway. Because of this abrupt change, we now have to ask more pointed questions to anyone who uses that word. What used to be agreed upon is no longer, and the culture continues to change around us whether we like it or not. As a response we could simply throw up our arms in exasperation, throw in the towel and say, "I'm done with all of this, I can't keep up!" Conversely, we could use these moments to reevaluate the words that we use and make sure that we are clear in our intentions, language, and definitions.

When a group like Merriam-Webster changes something as solid as the definition of a word that has been used in academia and culture for centuries, it brings to light just how important it is for us to be on the same page with our language. Because churches, denominations, and seminaries are constantly wrestling over theological and doctrinal issues daily, it is critical that we spend the necessary time dissecting these words and making sure our language reflects our intention and the heart of Scripture.

As our words go, so goes the culture.

Even Jesus had to deal with and adapt to this problem. In first-century Israel, the prevailing school of thought was that the Messiah would come and overthrow Rome and free them from their oppressive captors. When Jesus came, the people and disciples were asking him when he was going to establish his rule and wage a holy war against the oppressors. In stark contrast to that idea, Jesus told his disciples that he must die in order to accomplish what he came to do. So foreign and detestable was this idea that Peter told Jesus he wasn't going to let that happen, to which Jesus called Peter "Satan" and made the whole conversation a bit awkward. This all happened because they failed to understand the culture that Jesus came to change. It was the heart that Jesus was after. Once the heart was transformed, the culture around would be transformed soon after that.

This problem carries right through to our church cultures where many think that Jesus died on the cross so that people could go to church. Obviously, no one says this out loud but many of the systems, language, and celebrations all surround going to a building instead of being a people. The language of disciple-making needs to be such that people know that a disciple must trust, follow, and obey Jesus. This creates a culture that is outwardly focused on the Great Commandment and the Great Commission, rather than an inward focus of finding all we need in a sermon. The culture must shift from the "attend to be a disciple" model to the "go and make disciples" model.

Evaluating Our Language

For better or worse, your church has a culture. Every church has a culture. It could be an older church with a traditional liturgy or a new church that only embraces those with skinny jeans and a man bun. It could have a contemporary worship style, embrace the old hymns, or be non-instrumental. It is imperative to know our culture's language and what is being communicated through it. Evaluating our language, as it relates to our specific church or ministry culture, is a path many more pastors and leaders need to walk down. We must embrace the process of honest evaluation if we want to see any lasting change in our respective ministries. This process is known as adaptive leadership. Ronald Heifetz says, "Adaptive leadership consists of the learning required to address conflicts in the values people hold, or to diminish the gap between the values people stand for and the reality they face."[4] Adaptive leadership is the ability to pivot, change course, and adapt to an ever changing culture around us. If we fail to recognize that change is a constant thing we will need to deal with, we will have a hard time addressing the needs in a culture that has passed us by.

Please don't misunderstand me. I am not simply recommending that you get together with your team and draft a new mission statement or charter. Those are merely words on a page. I am not asking you to ponder these things for a moment in your heart and just pray about it. You don't even need to have a board meeting to understand what the Great Commission says. If you want to see God do a work in your midst. If you want to see lives changed before your eyes. If you want to see a new wave of the Holy Spirit changing lives, you will need to embrace new things. You will need to embrace a new culture that is defined by its adaptability to an ever changing world. A culture defined by doing what God has commanded and not just what tradition compels. A culture marked by intentional language, purposeful communication, and a mindset that knows Jesus called you to make disciples, not to build a church. Let me tell you what that path looked like for me.

A few years ago, I found myself in one of the craziest seasons of my life. The board at my church had just asked me to be the new lead pastor after the passing of our senior pastor. It was a crazy time dealing with various emotions over the loss of my pastor and friend and the new position of leading a large church and sizable staff. I served at my church for eleven years as an associate pastor, and I felt like a fish out of water thinking about the demands of this new role and season in my life. Knowing that the Lord was calling me to a new position, I was fearful and excited for this new chapter in my church and family life.

I am not sure everyone goes through this, but after the first few months of being the lead pastor, I found myself in what I would call a mid-ministry crisis. I didn't go out and buy a sports car or blow the church budget on something frivolous. In fact, it wasn't as crazy as you might think, and it wasn't anything that I was struggling with outwardly. I found myself faced with something I had never even considered. I understood the call to run the church as an organization. I understood the practice and business side of church leadership. I knew the fundamentals of how to preach and how to lead people. However, after doing it for a few months, a looming cloud came over me as I continually asked myself, "What am I doing? What type of church culture was I called to initiate? What kinds of things needed to change to facilitate this culture change?" I knew that there would be a different culture because there would be new leadership, but what is the process to make that happen in a way that would shepherd people well? Knowing how to run a church and knowing how to shepherd God's people are two vastly different things.

On paper, I was president and CEO of a corporation. I could hear the Holy Spirit saying, "Wow, look at you." very sarcastically in my heart. I really started to wrestle with doubts about the church's ultimate direction and the task before me. James 3:1 would often come into my heart and mind.

> "Not many of you should become teachers, my brothers, for you know that we who teach will be judged with greater strictness."[5]

This Scripture began to take on more weight as I pondered the things I was teaching and their implications with the culture that Jesus was calling me to cultivate. The questions continued to come. Over and over, I kept asking, "Are we making any difference in the Kingdom?" As someone who loves Jesus and the gospel, these questions were foreign to me as I usually exuded confidence in what I was doing, yet inside I began to question everything. So, I began to do what I knew to do. I began to pray and read the Word of God.

As I began to do this, the Lord revealed something that seemed like a secret hidden in plain sight through his word. *Make disciples.* The church existed, for one thing, to make more disciples. It may sound like a "Duh" moment, and it was. However, it was exactly what I needed to hear. Don't complicate it, don't overthink it. Go back to the basics and just make disciples of Jesus. Armed with this mission and charge from the word of God, I began to read everything I could about making disciples in the church and disciple-making as a whole. I even told a friend about what the Lord had shown me, to which he looked at me like I was telling him the sky was blue as if it was a new discovery.

But herein lies the problem that I was having. At our church, we *were* making disciples. Ask anyone at our church if we were making disciples, and I am sure that the answer would be a resounding "YES!" When I would tell people that we needed to get back to making disciples, they looked at me with that, "What do you think we have been doing for the last 40 years?" face. For a few weeks, I felt like a crazy person telling people we need to get back to making disciples. I was beginning to sense that I was failing to communicate precisely what the Lord was showing me. It wasn't until I explained what a disciple was in my mind that people started to see the problem that was taking place. Many people I talked to thought that the purpose of discipleship was only to develop people into weekly churchgoers or get them to serve in a ministry within the church. The kind of disciples that God was calling us to make were those who follow Jesus in every area of their lives, not just at church. We were all using the same words, but we passed each other in our meanings, like ships in the night. We all used the word disciple, but we meant different things. This may seem like a subtle shift in language, but this intentional move of getting on the same page with our definitions was about to have a huge impact on my team, and in the culture of the church I was called to lead.

It was at this point that I knew something big needed to change. Things were changing in my heart, but I needed to see an external change; I needed the change to happen in my life and in the life of the people that I was called to serve. God was calling me to pivot and shift the culture in our church. Not knowing the best strategy to get this accomplished, I reached out to another pastor and friend in my denominational tribe who had also taken over a large church about four years prior. He had much the same scenario in that he took over for a beloved pastor who had passed away suddenly. Upon getting him on the phone and letting him know my situation, he began to pour into me words that I needed to hear, rather than words I wanted to hear. He told me that changing a culture takes time and effort, so I need to take it slow. I hate slow. To those that know me as a leader, I am a proverbial gas pedal, so hearing the words "take it slow" was a bit of a shock to my system. Slow is not my natural pace. I am the guy who, when a good idea comes around, wants to implement it as quickly as possible. These words seemed foreign and counterintuitive. My friend gave me an illustration. "Dan," he said, "You are on a battle-ship, at war out at sea going 30 knots, all while turning and trying to retrofit the ship. You are going to want to take it slow."

As I pondered and prayed, the Lord again showed me some truths that I needed to hear.

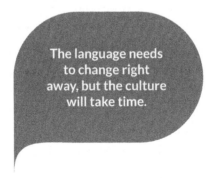

The language needs to change right away, but the culture will take time.

As you recall from my chapter on the gospel, I told the story of how Kodak failed to act quickly enough to shift to a digital photography business model, and it was their downfall. The failure to act quickly, adapt to the shifting market, and change strategy caused a ripple effect that bankrupted the company. In trying to expose the problem with the culture, we need to recognize that there are two problems to expose. The first is that sometimes we can lack the initiative and fortitude to act quickly enough when a culture change is needed. The second is when change is necessary, but we do it so fast that people cannot keep up.

There are roles that I have in my life where I function either like a gas pedal or a brake pedal. At home, I am a brake pedal. Whether I am talking my wife down from an emotionally charged moment, slowing our roll on a financial purchase, or admonishing my children to think and pray before they open their mouths, I am good at pumping the brakes in my personal life. However, I am a full-fledged, chrome-plated, LED gas pedal in my professional life. This is so true about me that we have a phrase amongst the pastors on our staff that says, "Let people catch up." I need to hear that phrase often because I have to realize that people won't be able to catch the vision if I am leading too fast. I have learned over the years that whether you are a gas or a brake pedal, you must keep this phrase in mind:

Shepherd people through change; don't make them victims of change.

Implementing Language Change

I am not going to sugar coat it; change is hard. It's hard because any change involves loss. Tod Bolsinger says in his book, *Canoeing the Mountains,* "Growth, transformation, and adaptation always means loss. Change is loss. And even experimental changes signal loud and clear that change and loss—is coming."[6]

I, for one, don't like to lose. I am sure you don't either. For some of us our identity is wrapped up in something that God wants to change. It may be a ministry we started long ago, or something that we told ourselves selfishly we would never change and now it is simply stubbornness and pride that keeps us from what God wants for us and our ministries. Because change involves loss, it can be hard for us to see the need to change, or we are so concerned about the potential blowback that we never move.

There are also parts of changing a culture that will be painfully slow. You can count on it. Shifts in a culture, especially ones that have been established long ago and have deep roots are going to take a while to change. This can be a good or a bad thing depending on your perspective. I remember in my old church switching from cassette tapes to CDs. There was a mini revolt. I remember the switch from CDs to everything being free on the internet where I was certain that some of the people affected were wondering if the devil simply sent me to torment them. There are people who just have a hard time shifting and adopting new ways, since the old ways had been a part of the culture for many years. Shepherd them through the change, don't make them victims of the change.

So where can you start? In my experience you are never going to be able to shift a culture if you are not a part of it. If you are an absentee pastor that rolls in once a week to deliver the word, you will never change the culture because you are truly not a participant in the culture. You must know the people and the community of believers that you minister to.

The second thing I would suggest is seeking perspectives that are different from your own. It is totally natural for us to surround ourselves with people who think and act much like ourselves. Hobbies, likes, and dislikes bring people together like nothing else. However, leadership that is focused on changing the culture will embrace different voices that see things from perspectives that challenge us in our own biases and presuppositions.

Thirdly, set goals. If you don't know where you want to go, you will never get there.

Set your sights on the culture you want to create and keep your heart, prayers, and mind focused on the task.

Put some posters or, at the least, some post-it notes around your space so that you are reminded all the time of what you are focused on doing.

A few weeks ago, I received an email for an open casting call for extras to be in a film that was recreating a scene from the Jesus

Movement of the late 1960s and early 1970s. They were making a movie about what Jesus did. The reality is I don't want to be in a movie about what Jesus did in the 1970s. I want to see the Lord do a whole new work in our midst. I want God to do something so radical that they will want to make movies about it in 40 years. I want a new work and a new move of the Spirit! But in order for that to happen, we must have leaders that are willing to do the hard work of evaluating our flawed language that hasn't produced much over the last few generations and have the intestinal fortitude to act with courage to create a culture conducive to disciple-making.

Cultures take a while to form, and they will take a while to change. That shouldn't scare you; it should prepare you for the long haul. Be intentional. Clarify your meanings. Say them a thousand times. And don't give up.

CHAPTER 5

PLAN

By Dan Leitz

"If you fail to plan, you are planning to fail!"
*~ **Benjamin Franklin***

This is the chapter that everyone wants to read because you hope it will answer the question that you and everyone else wants to know, "What's the plan?" You are looking for the answer, the steps, the layout, the method, the program – whatever you want to call it. Some of you might have even skipped the first four chapters just so you could get to the good stuff, get to the punchline. You just want the answer. I am sorry to disappoint you, but it doesn't work that way. I was disappointed too when I realized that there were no silver bullets in disciple-making. I know we all want one, but they don't exist. When Jesus told us to pick up our cross, carry it, and follow him, he didn't say it would be easy or that we would get a wheelbarrow to help take the load. Quite the opposite, he said it would be challenging, but he would give us his Spirit (John 14:15-17).

Having a plan for disciple-making is crucial to the local church. Disciple-making can no longer be just a buzzword or something we have on our websites to attract people who we think want to hear those words.

> The Great Commission isn't a marketing strategy. It is the template Jesus gave us to change the world.

It was late 2004. My wife, Nicole, and I were married in September of that year and were beginning the long journey of learning what becoming one really looks like. We were living in an apartment not far from the church I was working at as a high school teacher. My wife worked at a local coffee shop and as a piano instructor at a local music studio. We were both working hard in those early years, and making our relationship a priority in the busyness of life was very important to both of us. We both had good jobs when we married and we weren't struggling financially, as most couples do when they are just starting out. We were able to go out to dinner a few times a week and were living those first few years very comfortably.

One morning as I was heading out for work, my wife asked me what I wanted for dinner. She had the day off and planned to have dinner made for me when I got home. I told her very specifically that one of my favorite comfort foods was baked mac n' cheese. Baked mac n' cheese is a fantastic comfort food with a crunchy cheese top that, to this day, makes my mouth water. I wasn't super particular about the recipe as there aren't many ingredients to mess up, so I simply told her to find a recipe online and just make it. I found myself daydreaming throughout the day about getting home and having baked mac n' cheese. I couldn't have been more excited. When I got home, I could feel the warmth of the hot oven as I walked in. "This is it," I thought to myself, "this beautiful moment is what marriage is all about. I will have no trouble doing this for the rest of my life."

As we sat down at our small dining room table, I was cooing over the joy that I had found in this moment. My wife plated the dish, and my eagerness was off the charts. We prayed and dug in. Well, one bite in, and I knew something was off. My hopes and dreams of marriage were slowly eroding with every chew. Instead of the warm wave of comfort I had hoped would wash over me with every bite, I was greeted instead with a harsh, unappealing, yet strangely familiar flavor. Being newly married, I proceeded with caution, and said, "Hey babe, something tastes funny." My wife gave me a look that started with an "I don't know what you are talking about" face, which quickly morphed into a "disappointed that you noticed" face. My dear wife, bless her heart, proceeded to tell me how she got a recipe online titled, *The Best Baked Mac n' Cheese.* She thought it was a good start. I nodded with polite understanding. If it is titled the best, it must be *the best*! As she began to prepare the dish for my arrival, she gathered the items needed to make the dish. She told me as she was getting the supplies required for the recipe she discovered that we were out of regular cheese. Knowing that I would be home shortly, and there was no time to go to the store, she pulled out the only thing she had in the fridge, soy cheese. Yeah ... soy cheese.

Short backstory. My wife had struggled with a dairy allergy early in life and was not going whole-hog into dairy, so she had some dairy substitutes in the fridge. "Ahh," I said, as the compassion kicked in, "That explains the texture and the not-real-cheese flavor, but there is something else. Something tastes sweet." Looking down at the floor, she added, "We were also out of regular milk, so I substituted it with vanilla soy milk." My palm quickly found my forehead, as I exclaimed, "Seriously?!" This wasn't even close to baked mac n' cheese. This concoction was promptly dubbed *Very Vanilla Soy Mac n' Cheese* in the Leitz household. Please don't try this at home.

Needless to say, the rest of the night was filled with take-out food and some intense fellowship as we grappled with where we both went wrong. We learned a lot about one another that night. I wasn't specific about what I was looking for in the dish, and she realized that substitutes for the real thing will always leave you knowing that something is off or missing. I gave general direction and not specifics and I paid the price. She tried to cut corners and, to this day, it is the source of ongoing laughter in our home.

The same is true for making disciples. You can't just whip them up, you can't assume everyone knows what you mean by disciple, and you cannot substitute intentional relationships and community building with classes and sermons. You can't be vague about making disciples, and you can't cut corners and hope that things will turn out right.

> Hard work is a hallmark of discipleship, and you won't be able to skate your way through without being intentional with your language and having an intentional plan for disciple-making.

Exposing the Problem

When I was a kid in grade school, we had to use a tool from time to time throughout the school year known as an encyclopedia. If you are not familiar with this tool (cough, cough, I'm getting older), it was used for gleaning knowledge and information about history, people, places, and other historical elements of note. If you are over 40 years old, you too remember the encyclopedia. To get the desired information for a book, paper, or simply for knowledge, you would have to retrieve one of the large books, part of a 20-30 volume set, flip through the pages, and hopefully get the information you needed. However, in our culture today, with the internet, smartphones, and digital assistants, encyclopedias have been relegated to former things. They will someday end up in a museum about how things used to be.

In many ways, the advent of modern technology has produced access to masses of information, the likes of which were unimaginable in previous generations. You could have a random question that pops up in your head, speak to a digital assistant that is listening for you to ask anything, and within seconds have the answer to a question you had never even thought of before. We would have to count the cost of such thoughts and questions in the past. If you ever wonder, like I did the other day after watching a random YouTube video, why beavers build dams, you would really have to count the cost of finding such an answer. "Do I really want to pull out a reference book to find this information? If I can't find it there, do I want to take a trip to the library? If I can't find it in the library, do I want to call up a zoo or set up a meeting with a beaver expert to find out?" It's exhausting to even think about. Today, you just have to say your question out loud, and a virtual voice from a little speaker in the room will give you all the information you want to know.

All these advances in technology have undoubtedly made things easier, and the access to information more prevalent than at any time in human history. But it has had an adverse effect on us and the culture as well. What is this adverse effect, you might ask? To put it bluntly, it has made us lazy. If you have ever sat in front of a microwave lamenting the fact that your *Hot Pocket* takes all of 2 minutes to cook, you will understand what I am talking about. As a culture, we have gotten so accustomed to ease, turnkey, and putting in the minimal effort that we have neglected to adequately formulate a plan for what God is calling us to do. For some pastors and leaders, their plan is to see what the bigger church down the street is doing and emulate it to see if their model will give you the increase that you are looking for. Others plan to simply carry on the programs that the previous pastor had left and try not to rock the boat too much. Still, for others, the plan is merely to turn every directive in Scripture into a program or ministry in order to check all the boxes.

In the western church culture, we have relegated discipleship to a checkbox that needs to be marked off. We all know that the Great Commission is a mandate, and we all know we are supposed to be doing it, but not many of us can answer some of the most basic questions when it comes to the disciples we are supposedly making.

- What does a disciple look like?
- At what point does someone become a disciple?
- How do I know when we have made a disciple?
- Does a disciple know that they are a disciple?

If you can't answer these questions with certainty, I can tell you the people you shepherd or serve don't know either. And it goes without saying, you don't have an intentional plan.

Evaluating Our Language

So, what do we do? How do we fix this? As Bill Hull would often mention to me, "Don't announce the revolution, just start it." If you are like me and have been a part of many ministries and churches throughout your life, you have seen your fair share of ministry or program launches. I have seen countless ministries launch with great fanfare cookouts, potlucks, concerts, and festivals. They are all used to get people excited about something that is starting. Please don't get me wrong, none of those things are bad in and of themselves, but when it comes to creating a culture that centers around disciple-making, bigger isn't always better. On the days when there was a launch or kick-off party, one thing was always common; big numbers at the kick-off almost always ended with a trickle of people. Big fanfare, small results.

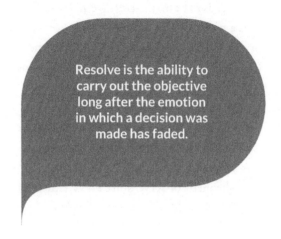

Resolve is the ability to carry out the objective long after the emotion in which a decision was made has faded.

Signup sheets, fanfare, and BBQ are not plans. They are a draw, but they aren't a plan.

As I told you back in Chapter 4, my mid-ministry crisis led me on a journey to reevaluate and examine the gospel I was preaching and how our church was doing at making disciples.

As I brought this revelation to a friend, he invited me to a conference that was taking place in just over a month. I quickly bought a plane ticket and knew that the Lord's hand of providence was all over my newfound passion. I knew that the Lord would give me the best material because our people deserve the best. Armed with an extra suitcase, I came to this conference determined to bring back the best books, ideas, and curriculum to my people so that our church could be the best at being disciples who made disciples. I started to buy everything. I was going booth to booth, stocking up on books and discipleship kits so I could take them home, ingest them, and pick the best one for the people of my church. Being a pastor of a large church meant that I would also have to hire a guy to be a discipleship pastor of sorts and take my plan to the streets. I was on a mission, and I could not be stopped. I had the Great Commission as my charge, the Holy Spirit as my fire, and I was zealous to make it happen!

As you can tell from my build, something happened. But it wasn't what I expected. Amid my buying fury, I came across a booth that was a bit unassuming. It was nice, but they only had one book. Most of the tables I saw had several books, work-books, boxed sets, etc. This table just had *one* book. One of the team members staffing the booth came over to me and asked me how I was doing and what I was looking for. I asked him if the book on the table was their curriculum. His response was less than convincing. "Kind of," he responded. As that was not the response I was looking for, I asked him a more pointed question, "What are you guys selling?" I wanted him to point me to the product table so I could buy what he was selling and move on to the next booth, buy more books, and get to making disciples. The kind man asked me again, "What are you looking for?" I told him my story and that I was zealous about making disciples. From the look on his face, I could tell that he had seen many like me before. He settled me down, began digging into my soul, and helped me begin asking the right questions to get started on the journey he knew I should be on.

Through a series of conversations that day, this man helped me see that having a stack of books wasn't a plan. He told me about the organization that he was with, called The Bonhoeffer Project, and convinced me to come to their breakout sessions to hear more. Over the next couple of days, I started realizing that my plan was to find a silver bullet, hire another guy to administer that silver bullet, and then call myself accomplished. I could already feel myself patting myself on the back.

I found myself on a breakneck speed journey of self-reflection and introspection. Within the span of two days, I experienced a wide range of emotions from self-confidence to questioning my calling as a pastor. I had a suitcase full of curriculum that now seemed useless. My plan was to launch another program, get sign-ups, and tell everyone it would be great. I was going to get people hyped up, and maybe hire a big named band to help me launch it. To this day, I have that stack of books sitting in a cabinet in my office to remind me of what we all try to do.

Having a plan for disciple-making is not something we can outsource, purchase, or hire someone else to do. Disciple-making is not a program, a ministry, or a campaign. It is not a course, a class, or a certificate program to be completed.

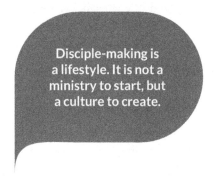

Disciple-making is a lifestyle. It is not a ministry to start, but a culture to create.

It is not a one-time event, but a lifetime of following and teaching others to do the same. Disciple-making is a revolution, one disciple at a time.

Implementing Language Change

Dallas Willard famously said, "Every church needs to be able to answer two questions. First, what is our plan for making disciples? And second, does our plan work?" Dallas admonishes every church leader to develop a plan and then test that plan to make sure it is working. This is why Jim and I believe so strongly in The Bonhoeffer Project (TBP). TBP isn't a curriculum or a turnkey plan for making disciples. It is a process we use to come alongside you and help you formulate a lasting plan that will make disciples for generations to come. Let me be clear, we are not against curricula. In fact, there are a great number of curricula out there, and almost all of them have the same great strategy to them. Scripture memorization, Bible study, fruits of the Spirit, and practical Christian living to help people trust, follow, and obey Jesus. What is different about TBP is that it helps you develop a long-term plan or strategy and implement one of these methods into your ministry or context. It also challenges you to examine the gospel you preach, as it will have a profound effect on the disciples you are trying to make.

One of the central and most overlooked aspects of the plan we develop is being intentional about our language. We could have the best plan in the world, but if people fail to understand it, or it is not clear, it will be all for naught.

Let me give you an example. About a decade ago, my wife and I used to teach conferences around the country, ministering to teens and young adults on dating and relationships. This conference was a big draw and got a bunch of teens, young adults, and parents excited about this subject and learning about these topics from a biblical perspective. We would typically do the conference on Saturdays, with a pre-conference for the parents the night before. It was a way to make the parents feel at ease and ask questions about the specific subject matter we would cover. On one particular Friday night, my wife and I had a couple come up to us after the preconference to ask us a specific question about a relationship their daughter wanted to be in. They were still reluctant to give her the green light. They began explaining the story and giving us details about the potential relationship, the specifics of how the friendship started, and the current status of their relationship. They went back and forth, giving various stories and details about the pertinent information to help us better answer their question. In their commentary to us, they would constantly use the word "dating ." After hearing this word several times, I knew it was a word I needed clarification on before proceeding. As they were winding down their questioning, I simply asked them to help us understand what they meant by "dating."

After looking a bit confused and wondering why the guy who was going to teach their kids the next day on relationships needed to know what dating meant, they responded. The husband started explaining dating as he saw it, with a holding hands, going out to dinner or a movie alone, a kiss goodnight, and having her home by 10 pm kind of vibe. As he was speaking, I couldn't help but notice his wife went from a nodding affirmation when they asked their question to a posture and look of slowly emerging horror as her husband gave his definition of the word "dating." When he finished his explanation, she looked at him with the "you have got to be kidding me" face. What could only be described as a moment of intense fellowship between them sparked before our very eyes. Her version of dating, I quickly learned, was more of a courting, floral length gowns, *Little House on the Prairie* type vibe. Needless to say, they did not see eye to eye.

With one question, I exposed the real problem in the question they posed to us. They did not see eye to eye because they defined "dating" differently in their heads. They were talking to each other (this is good). They were trying to come to an agreement on the boundaries for their daughter (also good). They were sending her to a conference on the subject (good again) while going to a pre-conference themselves to help with their parenting challenges and be invested in their daughter's spiritual and relationship growth (awesome). However, they failed to see that their biggest problem was that they had never explored what the other meant when they said the word dating. It wasn't until I asked one of them to define it for us that it exposed the fact they were speaking to one another but had missed each other completely. They were intentional about their communication and their daughter's growth, all the while not understanding one another because they did not see that they both thought something different in their heads.

The same thing happens with us when we talk to each other and develop a strategy for disciple-making, but we never explore or question what we mean when we speak these words. I challenge you to ask yourself and the people on your team, "What is our plan for making disciples?" If they cannot answer you, you actually have your answer. It is not that the answer needs to be elaborate, polished, or beautifully written. On the contrary, it needs to be simple, approachable, and understood by all. If no one knows what they are trying to make, then you and your team will never know if you accomplished your goal.

Start with the end in mind. Think about what a disciple looks like and the characteristics that a disciple of Jesus possesses and then work backward from there. If you begin with the end in mind, you will have the desired outcome as your focus and then be able to accurately assess if your plan is indeed working as intended.

CHAPTER 6

IMPLEMENTATION

Jim Thomas

Ok. First, some context. I have a wooden storage shed in my backyard (actually, two, but that is not relevant to this story). A couple of months ago, I went out to get something and when I picked up a plastic storage container, I realized that termites had invaded and eaten through about half of the floor of the shed. As such, I had to decide the future of the shed; repair, renovate, destroy, or buy a new one.

Once word got out about our dilemma, which seems to happen in the church world, a group of men from our church construction team agreed to come over and rebuild the foundation andlay a new floor for us. A few weeks later, I received a call that two of them would be coming by one evening to drop off some lumber for the project. A little while later, they pulled up with a truck and trailer. After the obligatory greetings and small talk, one of the men backed the trailer up to the shed to unload. The other man and I started walking toward him when I happened to look down and saw something in the grass. What I at first took for a fallen tree branch (we essentially live in a forest), was something very different. In a second's time, and by the grace of God, I processed the scene and realized that we were about to step on a 3 ½ foot copperhead snake. I held my hand out over the chest of my friend, as you would do for a passenger in a car if you were suddenly breaking. We both stopped, gasped, and slowly backed up (or was it fast? I can't remember). We then signaled to our companion at the shed what had happened and why we were not joining him.

Let me say this as clearly as I can. I love animals. Well, most animals. Spiders, scorpions, mosquitoes, and ticks might be exceptions. But living in the American south, you just learn to live with all of these. Even snakes. My basic philosophy before I moved here was that the only good snake is a dead snake! But now that I have been here a decade, I realize that there are "good snakes" and "bad snakes." The good snakes can still bite, but aren't venomous, and take care of rodents and many times will dispatch the venomous snakes. The snake in question falls into the "bad snake" category. It is venomous, dangerous to humans and other animals, and just downright scary! As such, a quick decision was made to send the snake on to wherever snakes go once a human separates its head from its body. Plus, once my wife was alerted to the situation, it was clear that if we were going to stay in our home that evening there was to be a permanent resolution to this problem!

So, the three of us began to formulate a plan to dispose of our scaly friend. Several options were discussed and employed including firearms, shovels, rakes, and concrete blocks (it was all very gruesome). In the end, after about an hour of planning and working the plan, we found success and I was able to sleep in my house that evening.

Exposing the Problem

Many of us know that disciple-making is the core command that Jesus left to his church, but few churches embrace it as the central call for their ministry. In essence, it is the snake in the grass! Ministry leaders work hard at keeping the foundation of their organizations strong by implementing outreach strategies, solid programming, financial "on-ramps" for people to support the work, and mission's opportunities. In the proper context, all of these are good things, but fall into what Will Mancini calls "the lower room." or the spaces where people emotionally connect with the church. The problem is that many times these are detached from the "upper room", which is "God's unique disciple-making vision for the church."[1] In other words, on our way to the lower room we keep running into Matthew 28:18-20, Mark 16:14-16, Luke 24:44-49, John 20:21, and Acts 1:8, and honestly don't know what to do about it since such a vision isn't driving what happens on the "lower floor." As such, we may need to respond in several different ways.

First, we might respond with fear. Snakes are dangerous! But so might be disciple-making! To embrace a vision for a disciple-making culture in your ministry context might change everything. It might result in confusion, conflict, and criticism. Fear was our first inclination when we ran into the snake. As such, one of our first strategies was to simply ignore it. The thought was, "If we ignore it, maybe it will just go away, and we can get on with our initial plan." The problem was that it never moved. It was still there, and after the reminder (ultimatum) by my wife, not unlike those inconvenient verses mentioned above, we knew we had to do something about it. But what?

Second, we may need to recalibrate our thinking. If we can't simply dismiss disciple-making, then what do we do? We need to think differently about it, especially as it relates to the gospel that we preach. In *Conversion and Discipleship: You Can't Have One Without the Other*, Bill Hull quotes philosopher Dallas Willard. Willard states,

> "For Evangelical Christians, turning around the ship of their social reality, and restoring the understanding of salvation that characterized evangelicalism from its beginnings in Luther and periodically after him, will be very difficult if not impossible. It would primarily be a work of scriptural interpretation and theological reformulation, but modification of time-hardened practices will also be required. Radical changes in what we do in the way of 'church' will have to be made."[2]

In other words, we must reinvestigate the biblical gospel and how it relates to Jesus' call to disciple-making. In doing so, we begin to ask the question, "What are we inviting people to?" Are we inviting people to make a "decision" about Jesus or into a life of following Jesus?[3]

Third, once we begin the "work of scriptural interpretation and theological reformulation" regarding the gospel and disciple-making, we will need to develop a process to lead people toward the goal of Jesus' command. We went through several different iterations of a plan to engage and ultimately dispatch the snake before we settled on a course of action. If you are serious about creating a disciple-making culture in your setting, you will walk through many versions of a strategy both before and after you implement it. In fact, if you are not constantly asking hard questions along your journey that causes you to pause and recalculate, you probably aren't putting much effort into it.

Fourth, we must work the process with patience. Disciple-making and creating a disciple-making culture is a process over a long period of time. Therefore, patience is a key virtue in reaching your goal. After our first attempt at resolving our snake problem, the snake did move. In fact, it moved underneath a large shrub, making it impossible to engage it in the open. This totally messed up our strategy. As such, we revisited point #1, ignore it and maybe it would be gone in the morning. I then looked up and saw my wife looking out the glass door and knew immediately that we must proceed. But how? We had to tweak our strategy to make it more effective when our context changed. Though some of the original strategy was retained, new, creative elements were introduced to accomplish our task.

Fifth, we must implement our plan. Bill Hull says, "If you don't have a plan, you don't really intend to do anything. And if your plan has no timeline, it falls short of actually being a plan."[3] In other words, we can get so enamored and excited about strategy and systems that we never actually put our "feet on the floor" and put our plan into action. When this happens, all disciple-making remains in the realm of the theoretical or the theological and not in the practical living out of the gospel in the lives of those we lead.

Sixth, we need to learn to celebrate the results and keep moving forward. Following the implementation and success of our plan, I have a great picture of the three of us doing a victory dance in the trailer. Over the course of the coming week, we shared our journey and victory with countless others (and each time the snake grew in length and ferocity!). But the shed still needed fixing, and the men came as planned and did a great job of restoring the floor. Similarly, we don't simply replace the "lower room" with "upper room" philosophy, but allow the purpose of the church, making disciples, to drive what the lower room looks like. In fact, once we address Jesus' vision for the church, it frees us to engage the ministry of the church in new and exciting ways.

Evaluating Our Language

To embrace the difficult task of implementing a disciple-making strategy in a local ministry is the high calling of ministry leaders. To not do so is to devalue and sideline Jesus' main commission to his church and to relegate its members to the humdrum life of religious participation and consumerism. In other words, the language of "plan" and "implementation" must be seen as a unit for an effective disciple-making process to happen in your context. Not unlike our encounter with the snake, you can make all the plans in the world, but unless they are able to be implemented in an effective way, you may just end up with a mess on your hands. But when you realize that you have either missed a major element in leading the people entrusted to you, or you have not implemented a sustainable plan, then something must change.[4]

Herein lies a key problem in the idea of implementation. Many pastors and ministry leaders are afraid to rock the boat, tip the apple cart, make waves, disturb the peace, challenge the status quo, or whatever other metaphor you might like to use. Admittedly, this is tough for several reasons. Many leaders have invested their lives in the systems and processes they have put in place within their organizations and to change it would not only call into question their strategies, but their character and their ability to lead. This is where humility comes into play. In Proverbs 22:4, Solomon says, "The reward for humility and fear of the Lord is riches and honor and life." In other words, for those who embrace humility and obedience to the Lord's commands, they will experience success and favor from God. That is why James says, "'God opposes the proud but gives grace to the humble.' Submit yourselves therefore to God. Resist the devil, and he will flee from you. Draw near to God, and he will draw near to you. Cleanse your hands, you sinners, and purify your hearts, you double-minded. Be wretched and mourn and weep. Let your laughter be turned to mourning and your joy to gloom. Humble yourselves before the Lord, and he will exalt you."[5] Though James is specifically talking about quarrels among Christians and wrong motivations in ministry, this can easily be applied to the idea of implementation. When leaders humble themselves before God, he will champion his cause through them. When they don't, he won't! And when it comes to implementing a disciple-making plan where there hasn't been one or where there is a failed one, a leader's humility, honesty, and obedience will go a long way and will produce substantial results.

When leaders evaluate what they have already implemented and see that changes need to occur, they must enter a season of evaluation. The knee-jerk reaction is to "throw the baby out with the bathwater" or grab onto the latest fad (including plans, curriculum, or nomenclature) in favor of moving toward a disciple-making culture and plan. But let me challenge you to pump the brakes. Take a moment to look at what is already in place. Once you know God's vision, have a desire to see culture change happen, and have begun to work on a plan, evaluate what is already in place that might lead you to your goal.

We still do Sunday nights at our church. Yes, I know that I am in the minority, and it might seem antiquated to gather a much smaller group of people for a separate worship service, but that is who we are right now. I'll never forget being in a conversation with a well-known ministry leader who helped plant one of the largest church networks in the world. He was asking me about our church, our vision, and what we do. When I mentioned Sunday nights, he quickly said, "Why don't you get rid of that?" The answer came quickly. I simply responded, "They are not ready." He looked a little confused, but I serve a church that was a church plant in 1828! You read that correctly; not 1928, 1828! As such, we always joke that we still have charter members who like to do things the way they have always done them! Of course, that doesn't make that right, or mean that we are always going to do things that way. It just means that I need to know my context well enough to lead them well. You see, implementing a disciple-making plan is as much about leadership as anything. And I would contend, leadership is a form of discipleship. If you are not leading people anywhere, you are not discipling them. If you are not discipling them, you are not leading them! As such, instead of getting rid of Sunday evening service (or the use of the name Sunday School, etc.), we simply repurposed those spaces to help us reach God's vision he has given us for making disciples. Instead of a three-song service with a "sugar stick" sermon, we have repurposed Sunday evening to do a lay version of theological training for our people. Instead of Sunday School being a typical surface-level Bible study, we are repurposing it to train our leaders to make disciples.

One of the exercises we have done with our pastoral staff helps us with the issue of perspective. Every so often, so we can see what guests see when they come on our campus, we go to the sidewalk in front of our church, turn around facing the opposite way, shift our mindset to that of a guest, and then turn back around. We then ask questions like, "What do you see?", "What is confusing?", "Where do I go?", and "How do I get there?" We then enter the building and continue to ask more questions about signage, cleanliness, ease of navigation, etc. (unfortunately, we can't evaluate people as we usually do this through the week, but it might be a good idea to do a similar exercise on a Sunday, or whatever other day the congregation gathers for more effective evaluation). What's the point? Well, if this kind of exercise helps us to better evaluate the guest experience, how much more should we walk from the "front door" through the building of our disciple-making process. When you do, I bet you will be surprised. I bet you will find things that are already leading you to your goal, though you may have to tweak them in some areas. I bet you will also find some areas of adjustment, reclamation, and some areas that need to be discontinued. So, take a walk! Evaluate what you are already doing as you evaluate implementing a more comprehensive or new disciple-making plan in your ministry.

Implementing Language Change

So, how do you introduce the language of implementation in the context of your ministry? There are several things that you will need to consider as you begin the process of implementation.

Start the Revolution. Many pastors and leaders have asked us the "How long?" question. This is really a two-part question. The first part regards the issue of how long before they announce that they are implementing a new vision and plan into their culture. Well, of course, this depends on the culture and having the wisdom to lead people well. A relative of mine once told me a story of a church they attended that did this the wrong way. With a desire to move from a traditional, Sunday School model of Bible study groups to an off-campus community group model, the leaders of the church spent much time coming up with their plan. I don't discount that their plan might have been the best thing for their church and for the growth of their congregation, but the implementation was horrific. One Sunday morning, without warning and without any preparation, they announced at the end of the service that all Sunday School classes were now disbanded and that they were moving to a community group model. On top of that, all members had been placed into community groups without their consent. The fallout was unbelievable! Many of the young families who had built deep friendships in the church and were now placed with others they barely knew, or did not know at all, simply left the church. This was both poor implementation of a plan and a poor leadership call.

So, how long do you wait to announce the implementation of a disciple-making plan? As Dan mentioned in Chapter 5, one of the mantras of The Bonhoeffer Project is, "Don't announce the revolution, just start it!" Now this sounds very militant in nature, but really it is more strategic. Should you ever announce the revolution? Of course, but what if you started it first? When we implemented our strategy in our church, I started with me. Because there was no history of intentional disciple-making or formal discipling relationships in the life of the church, I simply gathered about six men and began discipling them. Over the course of about a year to a year and a half, God did a mighty work. At that time, two of the men came to me and asked if they could leave my group and start discipling others. My answer was, of course, yes! They started discipling other men and men from their groups began to branch off and disciple others. At a men's event a year or two later, our Men's Ministry Leader asked all of our men's discipleship group leaders to come up on stage to encourage men to be in discipling relationships. When we did, we realized that all of those on stage found their gestation from that original group. As God did a work in the men of our church, our ladies began to see their husbands' and friends' lives radically changed and they wanted in too! By the way, we did announce the revolution. It was about three years into the process, but everything began by simply starting the revolution.

Work the Process. The second "How long?" question regards how long it takes for a disciple-making strategy to get traction in a local ministry. First, let me say that starting discipleship groups (D-groups, or whatever clever name you want to use) is not the same as implementing a holistic plan for disciple-making in your church. These critical groups can, and should, be part of that solution, but are not the solution in themselves. I want to be clear here, and reiterate something we've mentioned before: There is no silver bullet for making disciples in your church. Discipleship is both a partnership and a process. It is a partnership between the Holy Spirit and the individual believer, as well as between believers, for the purpose of character formation toward spiritual maturity, disciplines of the Christian walk, and serving as ambassadors of Christ in the world. It is also a life-long process of becoming more and more like Jesus in character and actions. Since this is the case, the process for making disciples is not a one size fits all proposal. As such, leaders must work the process of developing a holistic vision for disciple-making in every aspect of their ministry.

As I mentioned, it took three years before we announced the implementation of our disciple-making strategy. So, what did we do during those three years? We started the revolution, as was already mentioned, but we did so much more. As a ministry team, we intentionally began working on a plan to lead the people in our charge toward the vision God had given us. Our goal was to implement this plan in every ministry within the life of the church, from preschool to adults, from weekly gatherings to annual events, and from large group settings to one-on-one relationships. This took countless hours of prayer, strategy sessions with key leadership, multiple revisions and tweaks, and many failed experiments on the ground. So, what are some of the things we did? In our teaching and preaching, we began to implement the language of discipleship in all our contexts. Once we agreed upon the common language we would use in our plan, including that of the gospel, disciple, disciple-making, etc., we started to talk about that in every environment in our church. Second, we started to implement "test cases" of disciple-making language and activity in different areas to see the reaction of the people. Some immediately came on board and some resisted. We evaluated the risk/reward variables in each situation, made changes, and kept working the process. The amazing thing was that when we did formally announce the plan, it had already been going for close to three years, and our people saw it as normative to who we are and what we do.

Have Patience. This is one of the hardest things for ministry leaders to do in implementing change. But we must remember what leadership experts Ronald Heifetz and Marty Linsky say, "Leadership is disappointing your own people at a rate they can absorb."[6] When we don't, we risk blowing up the whole process because of our impatience. Patience is a virtue as it relates to being a fruit, or evidence, of the Holy Spirit's presence in us (Galatians 5:23). Therefore, it will behoove us to recognize that patience is a necessary and critical part in the disciple-making process and in implementing a disciple-making plan.

Keep the Vision out Front. As you start the revolution and begin to implement your plan, don't give in to the inevitable drift of ministry management. Someone, usually the senior leader, but not always, needs to keep the vision God has given you out in front. The vision acts like the plumb line for the implementation and success of the plan. Many of us who have implemented plans in the past can attest to how easy it is to chase rabbit trails or dead ends because they seem right at the time, but ultimately are deviations from the original vision. Remember, good can be the enemy of best, so keep the vision out in front as you implement your plan.

Another thing that I have experienced regarding keeping the vision out front is what I will call the "invitation paradigm." Many leaders forget that when they introduce a plan for the purpose of implementation, they are inviting others into this process for the first time. Therefore, even though leaders have been immersed in the philosophy, strategy, and roll-out of the plan, those they lead have not. As such, two things must happen to help create viability and ownership in the plan. First, leaders must start the conversation over with those they lead. People who are introduced to a new plan will inevitably bring their thinking and suggestions to the plan. Now, just because people bring their thoughts to a plan doesn't mean you have to start over from scratch, but leaders must be willing to answer questions and field suggestions that they most likely have already walked through weeks or months before. The good thing is that you have already processed some of these issues and can respond with experience and wisdom because you have navigated those minefields. Also, good leaders must be open to things that they might have missed and revisit the plan in light of what may make it stronger. Second, new suggestions or misunderstandings can make it easy to move from the original vision. Leaders must keep the vision out front, so that any suggestions or corrections may be accepted or rejected based on the vision.

Be Willing to Change Again. Flexibility is a key aspect of leadership and disciple-making in implementing a vision and a plan. If you think that your plan is the best thing next to chicken fried steak and mashed potatoes with sawmill gravy (hard to beat, by the way), and there is no room for improvement or adjustment, then you are limiting yourself, and God, in helping it to become all he wants it to be. After our plan was announced and we started to implement it in its totality three years after starting the revolution, we began to evaluate it in real time. Even though we had run some test cases leading up to implementation, we now got to see it working, or not working, in all its glory! As such, we began to discover some holes in our thinking and doing of disciple-making. Therefore, we began to make some changes. Some of them were significant and some were not, but the willingness to change helped us become more efficient and effective in how we make disciples.

I can hear some of you right now. Wow, this sounds like a lot of work! Well, you are correct, it's a ton of work. But it's worth it to implement a plan that is birthed out of vision and gives life to disciple-making in your ministry. Several years ago, I spoke at a couple of pastor events for The Bonhoeffer Project in the state where I live. In the passion of the moment, as I was calling people to a revolution of disciple-making, I heard these words come out of my mouth: "If you want an easy answer to your ministry issues, please don't do disciple-making or participate in The Bonhoeffer Project. But if you want to do the hard work of the Great Commission, please join us on this "long obedience in the same direction."[7] Have you had that moment when you questioned the thing that just came out of your mouth? I thought, "Did I just destroy everything we have been trying to do over the last hour?" But I stand by my challenge. Disciple-making and implementing a disciple-making plan is hard work, but I would not want to settle for the alternative.

CHAPTER 7

MULTIPLICATION

By Dan Leitz

Multiplication. It has become a buzzword in the Christian community as of late. If you are in the loop, you use the word multiplication because it sounds good and really puts a positive spin on things. But what do we mean when we say multiply? Does multiplication simply mean more people? Does it mean more butts in the seats or more ministries? Does it mean more excitement and more events? Do we use the word multiplication as a synonym for addition or do we use it to validate our approach? Does the word multiplication just give us a new buzzword to use as we navigate the numbers with a positive spin?

> If we don't use this word carefully and with great consideration for what we actually mean, we will end up focusing on building a church that is trying to have better branding than the church down the street instead of multiplying biblical disciples just as Jesus instructed.

The need to expose, evaluate, and implement when it comes to this word is critical, if we are to see tangible, Spirit-filled growth in our midst.

Exposing the Problem

About a decade ago, my wife and I purchased our first home. It was a small 1100-square-foot, single-story home in the suburbs of San Diego. Fully in the homemaking stage, my wife and I were buying all the necessary items to make this blank canvas our home. One of the items that was a sizable purchase for us at the time was a brand-new range. Thankfully for us, my in-laws decided to help us out and buy it for us. As they made the big purchase, I decided to splurge for the extended warranty because it wasn't that much more to add on five years of coverage. You can't be too careful these days. About six months after the purchase, I noticed that the digital display that also doubled as a touchscreen wasn't functioning correctly. I would often give it a good smack, and it would come back to life, but only for a short while. About a week later, the problem began to manifest itself more regularly. Several times a day the unit would simply beep, turn on, turn off, set a timer, you name it. My wife and I would be in the other room, and then randomly, the unit would beep, and we would have to run in to see if it had turned on the heating element. I called the manufacturer to explain what was happening and got a warranty fix in no time. As it turned out, and no surprise to us, the display unit was faulty.

Having had the unit fixed, we went about our lives not thinking about it again until about six months after the repair when the oven again began to act erratically. We called the technician, and he diagnosed it again with another faulty display. I wondered if I got a lemon of a unit or if the replacement parts manufacturer had produced a bad batch. Frustrated by this, I went online to see if anyone else had the same problem. After a few minutes of research online, I found my answer. An entire website had been created, dedicated to those who had the same problem we had, with the exact model of the range we owned. This website informed me that the unit had a design flaw. Evidently, if you used the back two burners, the heat emanating from them would cause the digital display to warp and become unresponsive in many cases. The irony was not lost on me that I purchased an oven that would stop working because of the heat it produced. I was blown away that a giant, well-known company, could be so careless to have made a product that was obviously never tested in a real-world situation. After four additional warranty calls and four more replaced displays, the company eventually decided to give us a credit toward a new unit.

Some of you may be thinking, what does a story about a faulty range have to do with multiplication. Let me explain. Seeing the unit in the showroom with all its features on display was fantastic.

It was bright, gleaming in the light, and ultra-clean inside and out. It had everything we wanted in an oven and a few extra features thrown in for that wow factor. It didn't have buttons; it had a digital touch pad. I love tech, so new things like this always get me excited. You make the purchase, plug it in, and bask in the joy of your purchase. Everything looks like it will work out, but lurking underneath all the beautiful stainless steel is a defective product that won't make it for the long haul. I got an oven with all the bells and whistles that a first-time homeowner could want, but the function of the range left a lot to be desired. It was doomed from the start to fail and flounder. It was a shiny piece of junk.

For many of us, ministry has the same lure. There are many shiny churches out there. Many ministries with all the bells and whistles. They look good from the outside but what is happening on the inside? What is being multiplied? The company made my range along with thousands of other ranges. They were sold all throughout the country and all of them had the same flaw. They were all mass produced with the same issue. They all looked good, but none of them functioned properly.

Idealism and practicality are two different beasts. Idealism looks from the outside and assumes, based on the exterior, that everything is as it should be. Practicality isn't as concerned about aesthetics but rather functionality and if it will work out when your family comes over for Christmas dinner. After over a year with that terrible range and all the hours spent trying to get it to simply turn on or turn off correctly, I longed for a simple unit that would just work as it was intended. I wanted a unit that functioned properly. I had a flashy unit that didn't do what it was designed to do. The manufacturer spent too much time making the oven look good and not enough time on it actually working correctly.

The war between what *looks* good and what *is* good plays out in Scripture after a very hard-to-swallow sermon that Jesus gives in John 6. Towards the end of John chapter 6, we see Jesus telling those who were following him that to follow him, they would have to eat of his flesh and drink of his blood. Some understood, and some did not. The disciples grumbled and debated what Jesus meant, while others simply got up and left. John 6:66 says, "After this, many of his disciples turned back and no longer walked with him." Many pastors and church leaders would be aghast with people making a b-line for the exits after a sermon in our modern culture. Today, some church growth experts would have told Jesus that he needed to soften his tone or round off the edges to ensure his sermon wouldn't alienate people. Many who followed Jesus stopped following him because his teaching that day was too hard.

Jesus wasn't playing the short-term addition strategy, but the long-term multiplication strategy. He didn't have a kick-off fish fry to get more people at his next sermon, and he wasn't trying to woo the masses. He was there to point people to repentance and his Kingdom. Jesus knew that there would be people who would reject him and his message, and we must understand that we will endure the same thing. Jesus' strategy wasn't to wow people, but to point them to the Father. In fact, Jesus' strategy would be mocked by most of today's pastors. In Luke 9, we see how Jesus sent his followers out to do some Kingdom recruiting. "And he called the twelve together and gave them power and authority over all demons and to cure diseases, and he sent them out to proclaim the kingdom of God and heal. And he said to them, 'Take nothing for your journey, no staff, nor bag, nor bread, nor money; and do not have two tunics. And whatever house you enter, stay there, and from there depart. And wherever they do not receive you, when you leave that town, shake off the dust from your feet as a testimony against them.' And they departed and went through the villages, preaching the gospel and healing everywhere."

Jesus told them not to take anything with them. They didn't need a worship band, matching tunics with their new ministry logo, and there wasn't a fog machine in sight. They didn't need all the bells and whistles. Jesus simply told them to go out in his power and authority and preach the Kingdom and heal. That was it. It was that simple. A few verses later, we see that word got out about what was going on with Jesus and his followers, and those coming to see what all the fuss was about were about 20,000 people. I will also assume that Jesus didn't preach a fluff message there either.

It is easy for pastors and church leaders to focus on the wrong things. We can focus on looking good and having all the aesthetics when that isn't what Jesus called us to focus on. Please understand me. There is nothing sinful about, or inherently wrong with, having bells and whistles, but that should not be our focus. My brother or sister, you are not called, asked, implored, or needed to build the Church. Jesus said that was his job (Matt. 16:18). What Jesus told us to do is make disciples (Matthew 28:19). And not just any disciples, but disciples that will go on to make more disciples. Paul reiterated this to Timothy in 2 Timothy 2:2 when he said, "and what you have heard from me in the presence of many witnesses entrust to faithful men, who will be able to teach others also."

> The problem we need to expose, and it will take some honest evaluation, is that we have looked to the wrong metrics for far too long and valued the wrong things as markers of success.

We have fallen prey to having something shiny but it isn't functioning correctly; something that looks good on the outside, but has no chance of success long term.

Evaluating Our Language

The question we must ask ourselves is, "What am I multiplying?" Are you multiplying a program, a structure, or even a church slogan? Are you trying to create attractions that bring people in, or are you focused on making disciples one at a time? You can multiply anything. Given enough time and resources, you can multiply many things! Jesus called us to multiply people. Have you ever been so busy and thought to yourself, I wish there were more people to do the work? There are times that I will look around and wish there were three of me to get this all done. Church ministry, outside ministry, four kids, homeschooling. I wish there were other people that could help lighten the load. I wish there was a mechanism or mandate from God that would help us reproduce ourselves so that more could be done in the Kingdom. Oh wait? There is, and therein lies the beauty of discipleship and, more broadly, multiplication. The question is, are you making more of yourself? Are you making more people that look like Jesus?

I have seen over time the ebb and flow of the local church. The church on this side of town has a really good kids' program, so many young families have started attending that church. Another church will begin a series on a hot topic or current event, and it will bring the numbers up. Yet another church just opened its new coffee shop and advertised it on social media to all the Christians in the area, trying to lure people from one sheepfold to another. That is not multiplication, it's addition. It's sheep swapping, pure and simple. It is a shifting numbers game where the Church isn't growing at all. It is simply moving around from one sheepfold to another.

> The Church doesn't grow when more people come to your church; it grows when more people meet Jesus and become more Christlike.

Just the other day, I was listening to a podcast where a prominent pastor spoke about how we, as pastors and leaders, need to bring more and more politics into the pulpit. The pastor and his co-host were going back and forth about the reasoning behind this urgent issue that they were trying to call attention to. In one of their pleas, the pastor began to speak of the explosive growth that his church experienced because he talked about politics every week. He implied that you should follow his recipe if you want to see the same type of growth in your church. "Thousands upon thousands are coming to our church now," he exclaimed. Knowing that the way he was speaking about it made him sound a bit like an "it's all about the numbers guy," he quickly softened his tone and said, "but it's not about the numbers." About a minute later, he began talking about how many people they had baptized and started throwing numbers around again. Big numbers. Thousands. Again, as he was saying this, you could almost hear his gears grinding. He quickly said, "it's not about the numbers, though."

Many of us go through this same dynamic at various points in ministry. Some even struggle with this on a weekly basis. Judging our success by how many people are in attendance is not what Jesus did, nor is it the primary metric we need to evaluate. The numbers are an interesting thing. As I often say, numbers aren't everything, but they are a thing. But what kind of numbers are we talking about? When we say we are multiplying, what exactly are we saying we are multiplying?

We have all gotten caught up in the numbers game. We talk about them when they are up as though we had something to do with them, and we talk about them when they are down as though God was doing some pruning, or we are going through a season of "blessed subtractions." We have all tried to go the humble route and tell everyone that the numbers are all up to God, and we don't worry about them. We repeatedly say this to will ourselves out of focusing on the numbers. Like it or not, numbers are an indicator of multiplication, but they aren't the only, or primary, indicator. The numbers are an unreliable indicator because if we don't know what we are trying to multiply we will never know if we are succeeding or not. Let me illustrate.

I remember one time in high school, I had done poorly on a test and was trying to figure out a way to conceal my less-than-stellar grade from my parents. They knew that the test had come and gone and that it was a big exam. I tried to stall for a while and tell them that my teacher hadn't graded them yet. My parents were very engaged in my education, and I knew that before long, they would contact my teacher directly. I came up with what I thought was a genius plan. I told my parents that I had gotten a "95" on the test. And I wasn't lying. I simply didn't mention that the "95" wasn't a percentage, but rather the actual number of correct answers I got on the test. Some of you may be confused as well. I left out the critical detail that my "95" was out of a possible 200; I had solidly failed the test, getting a score of less than 50%. But without providing this critical piece of information to my parents, I could make it look like I had done better than I actually did.

The same is true for us today in our churches. What are we telling people we are trying to multiply? What kind of multiplication are we excited about and getting other people excited about? How shall I put it? We could see massive growth in attendance and not see a single person surrender to Christ. We could see seats filled, tithing and giving up, and still not see multiplication. Why? Because we are seeing addition but not multiplication.

When evaluating our language, I believe multiplication is the area, more than any other, where our language is defined more by what we do than what we say. Multiplication is determined by what we celebrate and what we deem as successful. If you notice, Jesus didn't celebrate when 20,000 people showed up to hear him teach. He didn't look around at his disciples and say, "Hey guys, do you see my crowd size?" or "Hey team, this is what we are going for?" In fact, after they all showed up, he would often preach something hard, and people would leave. I believe this was his way of separating those who were there for the feels and the food versus those who were there to surrender and follow. Jesus never celebrated people just showing up. He would celebrate when people repented of their sins and followed him. He would celebrate life transformation.

My brother or sister, let me share with you a truth that we must hold on to.

> The Church doesn't grow when people come to church on a Sunday; it grows when people surrender to Jesus and are being conformed to his likeness and teaching others to do the same.

Implementing Language Change

Maturity and growth are not linear, nor are they a one-size-fits-all proposition. As we invest in the people that God has given

113

us stewardship over, we must not look at them in a cookie-cutter-fashion. God has created each person uniquely, and each comes with blessings and challenges. Each of the previous chapters have focused on one of many areas that need attention and intention if we are going to make strides toward Kingdom building. Each subject is a drop in the bucket that, over time, will begin to produce long-lasting and effective Kingdom fruit that will remain for generations to come.

At the end of the day, it really comes down to what we are trying to produce. Are we trying to create a flashy service that entertains people and teaches a message that makes them feel warm inside, or are we aiming to preach the Truth and let God do with it what he will? Are we trying to attract people with flair and the feels, or are we seeking total life transformation because of the work of the Spirit in the lives of individuals? Are we trying to create people a mile wide and only an inch deep, or are we preparing them to be the Church and equip *them* for the work of ministry?

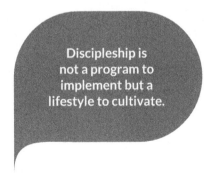

Discipleship is not a program to implement but a lifestyle to cultivate.

It is not about a series of checkboxes and books, but life transformation that leads to more and more fruitfulness. The multiplication that we need to celebrate in our churches and homes needs to reflect the diminishing flesh and the growing fruits of the Spirit. Paul tells us plainly what these are, and how the Spirit will help us grow in Christlikeness. Galatians 5:16-23 says, "But I say, walk by the Spirit, and you will not gratify the desires of the flesh. For the desires of the flesh are against the Spirit, and the desires of the Spirit are against the flesh, for these are opposed to each other, to keep you from doing the things you want to do. But if you are led by the Spirit, you are not under the law. Now the works of the flesh are evident: sexual immorality, impurity, sensuality, idolatry, sorcery, enmity, strife, jealousy, fits of anger, rivalries, dissensions, divisions, envy, drunkenness, orgies, and things like these. I warn you, as I warned you before, that those who do such things will not inherit the kingdom of God. But the fruit of the Spirit is love, joy, peace, patience, kindness, goodness, faithfulness, gentleness, self-control; against such things there is no law."

Paul tells the Galatian church, and us, that when we are in the Spirit, the works of the flesh diminish and the works of the Spirit increase. He is telling us the attributes of Christlikeness we need to pursue and reflect on an ongoing and ever-growing basis. The multiplication that we must strive for is a byproduct of the work of the Spirit in the life of every disciple that seeks to be like Jesus.

AFTERWORD

Jim Thomas

Watch your language!

If you have lived any life at all, someone has said this to you, and you have probably said it to someone else. Though this phrase is usually associated with some negative word, phrase, or idea, it is also a great reminder of what we are to do as we think through the language we use that both informs and guides how we do life and relationships. As we said in the introduction of this book, language is the currency of life, and we must be vigilant in exposing the problems with our language, evaluating the words, phrases, and concepts we use, and implement intentional and effective language in the pursuit of "world revolution through local movements of disciple-making".[1]

An example might be helpful to bring this idea to life. I was in 8th grade. I had just moved to a new, large school in a north suburb of Dallas, Texas from a small suburb of Jackson, Mississippi (a culture shock for sure). As any middle school boy would do, I was navigating the waters of the social dynamics of my prepubescent world, trying to make friends, and fit it the best I could. For some reason, maybe because I was the new kid, I became the target for several of the bullies in the school. They would incessantly make fun of me and point me out in negative ways for no reason. Because I was a somewhat compliant child (at least at that point in my life), I simply took the afront and abuse, not wanting to escalate situations or make waves and become more of an outcast than I already was.

One day, I was walking to the gymnasium for basketball practice, when I sensed a presence behind me. One of the bullies had seen me walking and sought me out for the daily round of taunting. His voice was grating, degrading, and loud. I felt the dark cloud of chastisement growing over my shoulders as he got closer. Suddenly, I felt a hand on my back as his words were accompanied with a push. I stumbled forward trying to keep my balance. When I recovered my steps, and out of sheer frustration and anger, I turned to face him. He stopped, smiled, and launched another witty remark from his arsenal. I had finally had enough. I said, "Shut up!" I know it wasn't the most intelligent or cutting thing I could have said, but it was all I had. His smile disappeared. His eyes narrowed. His lips pursed. And he responded, "Make me!" (This is high drama, huh?).

It came out of my mouth before I knew it. It flew like an arrow meant to destroy. Honestly, I didn't even weigh the potential impact of my words, but just let them fly. I responded with all the 8th grade swagger I could muster, "I don't make trash, I burn it!" (Yeah!!!!).

The next few minutes were a blur. All I remember was being lifted off the ground and shoved up against a cinder block wall. I was suspended about six inches off the ground with the bully's hand grasping the collar of my clothes. In that moment, I realized the size, weight, and strength of my opponent. I wondered in that brief moment what my parents would say about me at my funeral. Would I be championed as the underdog, a loving child who was the victim of undue cruelty and criminal behavior? Or would they vilify me as an idiot for taking on a bully much bigger than myself. Would I be seen as the rebel soldier in the hands of Darth Vader in the opening of *Star Wars: A New Hope* or Marty McFly in *Back to the Future* when he was called "chicken?"

What happened next was anything but expected. Having closed my eyes in anticipation of the inevitable punch, I opened them up to face my fate like a man (or as much of one as I was at the time). To my surprise, the bully had tears in his eyes and on his cheeks. He looked at me with all the hurt, pain, and vitriol of someone who had walked a rough road in his young life. With all he could muster, he simply said, "I am not trash!" He then let me down and walked away.

That day, I learned a lifelong lesson. Words matter! In my attempt at self-defense, I did not mean to call him "trash," I simply wanted to insult him as he had insulted me. I really didn't care what I said. But in that moment, I saw the pain of a life lived as someone considered "less than," which was probably one of the reasons he was acting the way he did. And it shaped me forever.

I am reminded of some words Jesus said to someone society considered less than. In Luke 18, Jesus was passing outside of the old city of Jericho when a blind beggar, named Bartimaeus, called out for his attention. The crowd warned him to be quiet, but he continued to call out all the more. Then two fateful words changed this man's life. Luke simply says, "Jesus stopped." He approached the man and asked, "What do you want me to do for you?" The man said, "Lord, I want to see." Seeing his faith, Jesus heals him, citing his faith, and the man begins to follow him, glorifying God. Amazingly, the crowd who had tried to shut the man up, also began praising God.

Words have power! They have the power to instruct or destruct, the power to edify or vilify, and the power to heal or hurt. Will you stop long enough to expose, evaluate, and implement words that move people toward deeper discipleship? Will you do the hard work of sorting through your current language, in light of Scripture, and clarifying what you are saying and why you are saying it? Remember, the gospel you proclaim will determine the disciples you produce. Your language plays a huge role in both the gospel you share and the disciple-making plan you implement in your ministry. When you pay attention to the language of disciple-making, we believe that you will see God do amazing things in the lives of individuals and churches.

ENDNOTES

Introduction

[1] Genesis 1:3-30, Christian Standard Bible (CSB).
[2] Lena Boroditsky, "How Language Shapes the Way We Think," Ted Talks, TEDWomen, Nov. 2017, https://www.ted.com/talks/lera_boroditsky_how_language_shapes_the_way_we_think.
[3] Proverbs 23:7, New American Standard Version (NASB).
[4] Matthew 28:19-20a, CSB.

Chapter 1- Gospel

[1] 1 Corinthians 15:14
[2] Scot McKnight, *The King Jesus Gospel*, revised edition (Grand Rapids: Zondervan, 2011).
[3] Bill Hull, *Conversion & Discipleship*, Zondervan, 2016
[4] John 9:4

Chapter 2- Disciple

[1] Dallas Willard, *The Great Omission: Reclaiming Jesus's Essential Teachings on Discipleship* (New York: Harper One, 2006), 5.
[2] Ibid, 6.

[3] Dallas Willard, *The Divine Conspiracy: Rediscovering Our Hidden Life in God* (New York: Harper One, 1997), xv.
[4] Bill Hull, *Conversion and Discipleship: You Can't Have One Without the Other* (Grand Rapids, MI: Zondervan, 2016), 232.
[5] Tim Keller, *The Prodigal God: Recovering the Heart of the Christian Faith* (New York: Dutton, 2008), 123.
[6] Hull, 38.

Chapter 3- Vision

[1] Psalm 8:3-8.
[2] 2 Corinthians 5:17-18.
[3] Revelation 21:5.
[4] Daniel Im. *No Silver Bullets.* (Nashville: B&H Publishing Group, 2017), p. 13-14.
[5] Proverbs 29:18.
[6] Tremper Longman III. Proverbs (Baker Commentary on the Old Testament Wisdom and Psalms). Grand Rapids, MI: Baker Publishing Group, 2006), p. 507.
[7] Tim Keller, *Center Church: Doing Balanced, Gospel-Centered Ministry in Your City* (Grand Rapids, MI: Zondervan, 2012), 17,18,19.

Chapter 4- Culture

[1] Andy Crouch, *Culture Making*, 191-192.
[2] J.R. Woodward, *Creating a Missional Culture*, 20.

[3] https://www.vox.com/identities/2020/6/10/21286656/merriam-webster-racism-definition

[4] Ronald Heifetz, *Leadership Without Easy Answers*, 22.

[5] James 3:1

[6] Tod Bolsinger, *Canoeing the Mountains*, 122.

Chapter 6- Implementation

[1] Will Mancini, *Future Church: Seven Laws of Real Church Growth* (Grand Rapids, MI: Baker Books, 2021), 22-29.

[2] Dallas Willard, Spiritual Formation as a Natural Part of Salvation, talk given at Wheaton College in 2008 quoted in Bill Hull, *Conversion and Discipleship* (Grand Rapids, MI: Zondervan, 2016), 22, emphasis added.

[3] Bill Hull, *Conversion and Discipleship: You Can't Have One Without the Other* (Grand Rapids, MI: Zondervan, 2016), 211.

[4] This is a key component of The Bonhoeffer Project which is covered over four cohort sessions. For more information on how to join a cohort, go to www.thebonhoefferproject.com.

[5] James 4:6-9 (ESV)

[6] Ronald Heifetz and Marty Linsky, *Leadership on the Line: Staying Alive Through the Dangers of Leading* (Boston, MA: Harvard Business Press, 2022), 142.

[7] From Eugene Peterson's book of the same name.

Afterword

[1] A main maxim in The Bonhoeffer Project. For more information on how you can enter into a process with other pastors/ministry leaders in forming not only the language of disciple-making, but a biblical understanding and plan for disciple-making in the specific context of your church or ministry, go to www.thebonhoefferproj-ect.com to join a cohort today.

The
GOSPEL YOU PROCLAIM
determines the
DISCIPLES YOU PRODUCE

WHY: THE GOSPEL
Change Your *Mind*
With all the incomplete, or false, "gospels"
circulating in the world today, we're equipping
leaders to put the gospel of discipleship first.

WHAT: MAKE DISCIPLES
Change Your *Heart*
The Kingdom of God is a world-wide
movement, and by investing into one person at
a time, you can change the world.

HOW: THE PLAN
Change Your *Behavior*
Everyone needs a plan in order to make
disciples. Through our process, you will walk
away with an actionable plan.

The Language of Disciple-Making	The Disciple's Guide to Choose the Life	Experience the Life Series
Dan Leitz & Jim Thomas	Bill Hull	Bill Hull & Paul Mascarella

Made in the USA
Monee, IL
01 August 2023

40291701R00080